About the book

There are 18 GCSE Mathematics higher papers and answers in this book. These are 6 sets of papers 1, 2 & 3 written as practice papers for GCSE Mathematics Higher Examination. Papers are mainly focusing on Edexcel, AQA & OCR GCSE examinations as well as other similar examination boards.

These papers are written according to the new grade 9-1 syllabus and questions are potential questions for the GCSE mathematics examinations. There have only been exams with this syllabus since June 2017. These 18 papers were written in a similar theme to those exams.

All the questions in this book are written by the author and they are new questions written purely to help and experience the students to prepare and test themselves for the GCSE mathematics higher exams.

Answers, solutions and mark schemes are included in this book. However, if you need to check your solutions, I advise you to ask your school mathematics teacher or your private mathematics tutor to mark your answers.

There are 5 sections to this book A, B, C, D, E & F. Each section contains 3 papers. First paper of each section is a non-calculator paper and second & third are calculator papers.

GCSE Mathematics Potential Papers

for grade 9 to 1 syllabuses by Edexcel, OCR & AQA includes answers

Higher level

By Dilan Wimalasena

Contents

Section A

GCSE Mathematics
Paper 1
(non-calculator)

Higher
Tier

Potential Paper A1

You must have: Ruler graduated in centimetres and millimetres, protractor, pair of compasses, pen, HB pencil, eraser.

Calculator is not allowed

**Time allowed
1 hour and 30minutes
Total 80 marks**

Name

Date

1. Solve the following inequality.

$$-11 \leq 2x - 3 < 1$$

(3 marks)

2. Work out the highest common factor & the lowest common multiple of 144 & 192.

(4 marks)

3. Andrew, Bruno & Corey shared £x in the ratio $y: 5: 9$. Corey has £90 more than Andrew & Bruno has £30 less than Andrew. Work out the values of x & y.

(4 marks)

4. *a*) Write the following numbers in standard form.

i) 407,000

(1 mark)

ii) 0.0407

(1 mark)

b) Work out the following and write the answer in standard form.

$$(2.5 \times 10^5) \times (5 \times 10^{-8})$$

(3 marks)
(total 5 marks)

5. Work out the sum of the interior angles of a nonagon.

(2 marks)

6. Cube A has a volume of $64cm^3$ & Cube B has a surface area of $216cm^2$.
   Work out ratios of their lengths.
   Give your answer in the form $a:b$ where a and b are integers.

(5 marks)

7. $y = x^2 + 5x + 2$

   i)   Complete the tale of values for $y = x^2 + 5x + 2$.

x	-5	-4	-3	-2	-1	0	1	2
y								

(2 marks)

   ii)   On the grid, draw the graph of $y = x^2 + 5x + 2$ for values of x from -5 to 2.

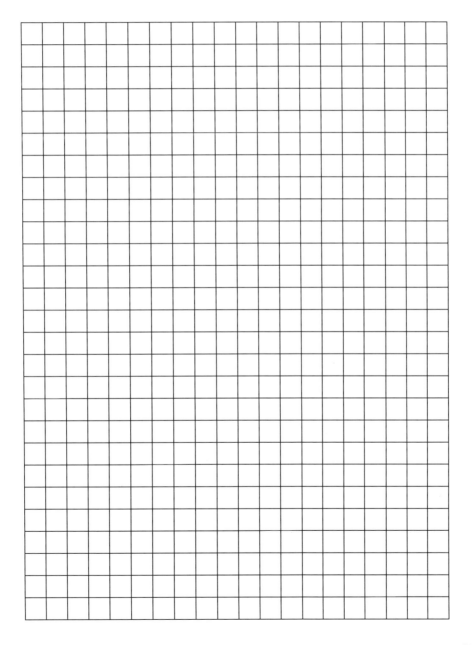

(3 marks)

(total 5 marks)

8. Work out the mean mark.

Marks	Frequency		
20-40	3		
40-60	5		
60-90	11		
90-100	1		

(4 marks)

9. A sphere has a surface area of $144\pi \ cm^2$. Work out the volume of the sphere in terms of π.

(4 marks)

10. Show that

$$0.0\dot{9}\dot{4} = \frac{47}{495}$$

(4 marks)

11. The salary structure of a company is summarised below.

Salary (£)	Frequency	
400-500	6	
500-600	11	
600-700	8	
700-800	5	
800-1000	2	

Using a cumulative frequency curve work out the median salary and the interquartile range for the salaries.

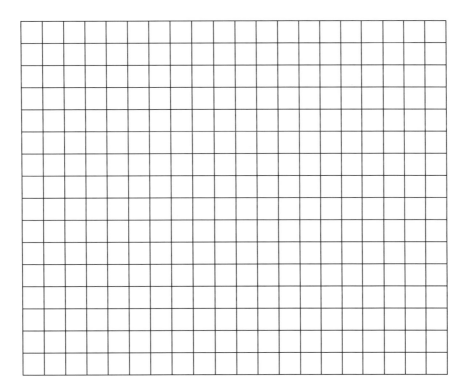

(6 marks)

12. Neil has 0.1 chance of being late to work. Work out the probability of Neil being late exactly once in two consecutive days.

(4 marks)

13. A train accelerates from rest to $30m/s$ in 12 seconds. A car accelerates from $11m/s$ to $33m/s$ in 10 seconds. Which of the two has the greater acceleration?

(5 marks)

14. OABC is a parallelogram. The vectors $\overrightarrow{OA} = 2a$ & $\overrightarrow{OC} = 4c$. The points P & Q are such that P is the midpoint of AB and $CQ: QB = 1:3$.

Work out the vector $\overrightarrow{PQ}$ in terms of a & c.

(6 marks)

15. y is directly proportional to x^2. When $y = 108, x = -6$. Work out

i) y when $x = 4$

(3 marks)

ii) x when $y = 147$

(3 marks)
(total 6 marks)

16. Work out the value of

$$3\frac{2}{5} \div \left(4\frac{1}{2} - 3\frac{7}{10}\right)$$

You must show all your working.

(5 marks)

17. Solve the following equation.

$$\frac{6}{5-x} + \frac{5}{1-4x} = 2$$

(4 marks)

18. A circle has centre $C(1,3)$ and passes through the point $P(13,8)$.
Work out the equation of the tangent to the circle at P.

(4 marks)

Total for paper: 80 marks

End

GCSE Mathematics
Paper 2
(calculator)

Higher
Tier

Potential Paper A2

You must have: Ruler graduated in centimetres and millimetres, protractor, pair of compasses, pen, HB pencil, eraser.

Calculator is allowed

Time allowed
1 hour and 30minutes
Total 80 marks

Name

Date

1. a) Simplify

$$\frac{(x^5)^4 \times (x^6)^3}{(x^3)^3 \times (x^6)^2}$$

(3 marks)

b) Expand and simplify the following expressions

i) $(4x - 5)(7x + 2)$ ii) $(2y - 3)^2$

(4 marks)
(total 7 marks)

2. $f(x) = x^2 - 2x - 3$

Sketch the graph of $y = f(x)$ clearly showing coordinates of points intersecting with the axes.

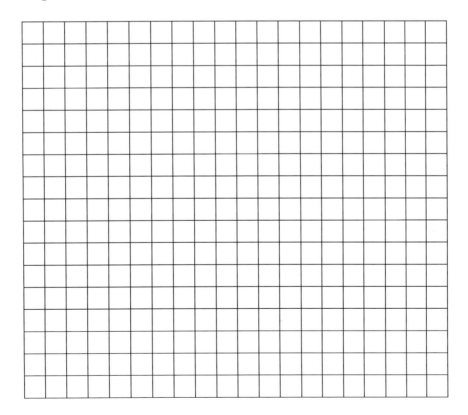

(3 marks)

3. $P = 200$ (correct to 1 significant figure)

    $Q = 13.7$ (correct to 1 decimal point)

    Calculate the following to 3 significant figures.

    i) the upper bound of $(P - Q)$

(2 marks)

    ii) the lower bound of $\dfrac{PQ}{P - Q}$

(3 marks)
(total 5 marks)

4. The points A & B are such that $A(1, -4)$ & $B(5,6)$. Work out the equation of the perpendicular line to AB through the midpoint of AB.

(5 marks)

5. A computer is £625. The value of the computer depreciates by 35% a year. Calculate the value after 4 years.

(2 marks)

6. A tablet is £550 in the UK and 23,999 Thai Baht in Thailand. Boris says the tablet is cheaper in Thailand. Is he correct?

$£1 = 42.35 \, Thai \, Baht$

(3 marks)

7. y is inversely proportional to x^2. When $y = 32, x = -3$.
Calculate

     $i) \, y \, when \, x = 4$ $ii) \, x \, when \, y = 2$

(5 marks)

8. $A(2,4), B(6,4)$ & $C(6,2)$

    i.   Plot the triangle ABC.

    ii.   Plot the enlargement of triangle ABC about the centre origin.

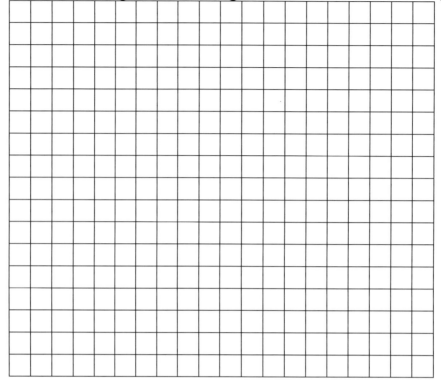

(5 marks)

9. Freddy asked 30 people which fruit they like from Apple, Banana and Cherry.

All 30 people like at least one of the fruits

2 people like all three

5 like apple and banana but not cherry

5 like apple & cherry

4 like banana and cherry

15 people like banana

3 people like only cherry

Freddy selects at random one of the 30 people. Calculate the probability that this person likes Apple.

(4 marks)

10. A sphere has radius 3cm. The sphere has the same surface area as a solid cylinder with height 6cm and radius r cm.

    i)   Show that
$$r^2 + 6r - 18 = 0$$

(3 marks)

    ii)   Hence, work out the value of r to 3 significant figures.

(3 marks)

(total 6 marks)

11. Work out the value of the angle ABC.

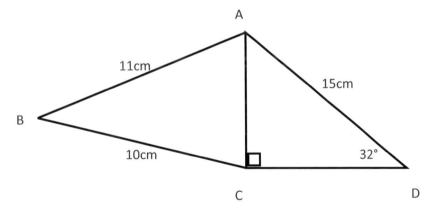

(5 marks)

12. $f(x) = 2x - 1$ & $g(x) = 3x + 2$

   i)   Work out
          $a)\ fg(1)$

(2 marks)

          $b)\ f^{-1}(x)$

(2 marks)

   ii)   Solve the equation

$$f^{-1}(x) = fg(1)$$

(2 marks)
(total 6 marks)

13. Prove that the opposite angles in a cyclic quadrilateral add up to $180°$.

(4 marks)

14. Solve the following quadratic inequality.
$$3x^2 - 2x - 8 > 0$$

(4 marks)

15. A bag has x apples. 2 of them are green and the rest are red. John ate two apples at random. The probability of him eating 2 green apples is $\frac{1}{10}$.

Work out the value of x.

(6 marks)

16. Solve the following quadratic simultaneous equations.

$$x^2 + y^2 = 90$$
$$y - 2x = 3$$

(6 marks)

17. Prove that the sum of any two odd integers is always even.

(4 marks)

Total for paper: 80 marks

End

GCSE Mathematics
Paper 3
(calculator)

Higher
Tier

Potential Paper A3

You must have: Ruler graduated in centimetres and millimetres, protractor, pair of compasses, pen, HB pencil, eraser.

Calculator is allowed

Time allowed
1 hour and 30minutes
Total 80 marks

Name

Date

1. Work out the lengths AC& AB.

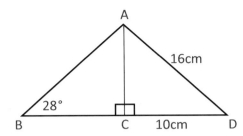

(4 marks)

2. $x = 2.7, y = -6.1 \ \& \ z = -3.2$
Work out the following to 3 significant figures.
$i) \ x - y - z^2$

(2 marks)

$ii) \dfrac{y^2 - 4z}{x^2}$

(2 marks)
(total 4 marks)

3. Make x the subject of the formula
$$y = \frac{2x + 5}{3x - 1}$$

(4 marks)

4. A computer is £740. The value of the computer decreases by 45% a year. Calculate the value at the end of the 5th year.

(3 marks)

5. Draw a frequency polygon for the following data.

Salaries (£)	Frequency
200-300	8
300-500	10
500-800	7
800-900	3
900-1000	1

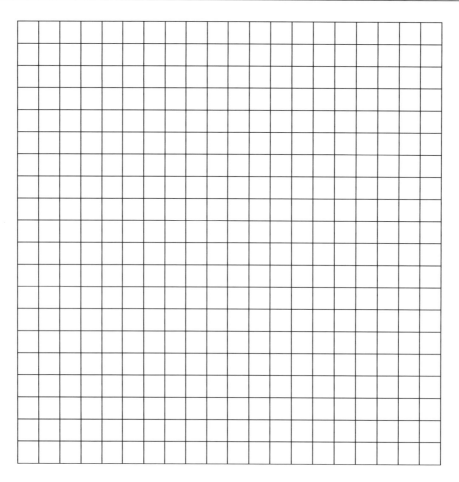

(3 marks)

6. A car travelled from A to B on a straight line. The speed of the car at A is $12m/s$ and the speed at B is $30m/s$. The car took 9 seconds to travel from A to B.

   Calculate acceleration of the car.

   (3 marks)

7. The area of the trapezium is equal to the area of the triangle. Calculate the value of h.

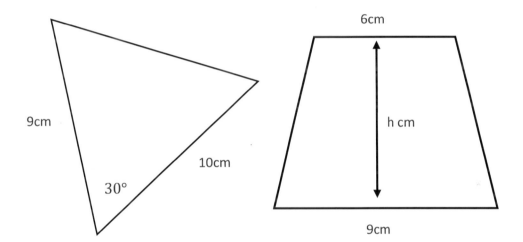

   (5 marks)

8. Mike runs a delivery company. He has a fixed charge of £5.75 plus £1.35 per mile. John paid a delivery charge of £21.95. Calculate the number of miles for Johns' delivery.

(3 marks)

9. Solve the following equation.

$$16^{x-2} \times 8^{x+1} = 32$$

(5 marks)

10. There are 5 colours. Andrew wants to pick two colours at random. Work out the number of colour combinations available to choose.

(3 marks)

11. Work out the value of x.

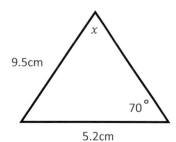

(3 marks)

12. Factorise the following expressions fully.

   $i)$ $18x^3 - 2x$ $ii)$ $2x^2 - 11x - 30$

(5 marks)

13. Prove that the triangle PQR is similar to the triangle PTS and hence, work out the length of the side RT.

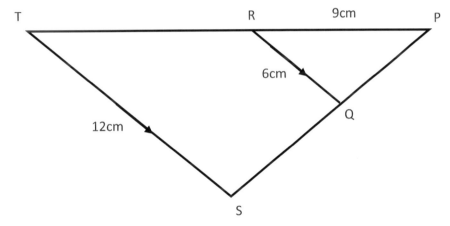

(5 marks)

14. The area of a rectangle is $150cm^2$ correct to 2 significant figures & the length of the rectangle is $18cm$ correct to the nearest centimetre. Calculate the lower bound for the width of the rectangle.

(4 marks)

15. A cube with length $10cm$ is drawn below.

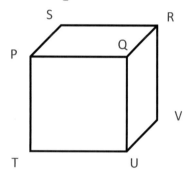

Calculate the angle $P\hat{R}T$ to one decimal place.

(6 marks)

16. Draw a histogram for the following data.

Marks	Frequency		
20-50	3		
50-70	6		
70-80	5		
80-100	2		

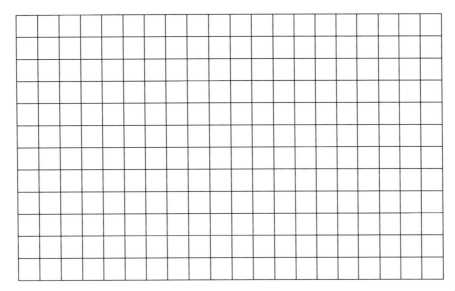

(4 marks)

17. The functions f & g are such that

$$f(x) = \frac{x-1}{2} \ \& \ g(x) = 4x - 5$$

Solve the equation $gf(x) = f^{-1}(3)$

(5 marks)

18. $f(x) = x^3 - 13x - 20$

   i)   Show that $f(x) = 0$ has a solution between $x = 4$ & $x = 5$.

(2 marks)

   ii)   Show that $f(x) = 0$ can be rearranged to
$$x = \sqrt[3]{13x + 20}$$

(2 marks)

   iii)   Using the iterative formula
$$x_{n+1} = \sqrt[3]{13x_n + 20} \text{ & } x_0 = 4.5$$

   Work out the values of x_1 & x_2.

(2 marks)
(6 marks)

19. Solve the following simultaneous equations.

$$xy = 48$$
$$y - 3x = 7$$

(5 marks)

Total for paper: 80 marks

End

Section B

GCSE Mathematics
Paper 1
(non-calculator)

Higher
Tier

Potential Paper B1

You must have: Ruler graduated in centimetres and millimetres, protractor, pair of compasses, pen, HB pencil, eraser.

Calculator is not allowed

Time allowed
1 hour and 30minutes
Total 80 marks

Name

Date

1. Work out

$$3\frac{1}{2} \div (4\frac{2}{5} - 2\frac{3}{4})$$

(4 marks)

2. Work out the percentage increase from 180 to 216.

(3 marks)

3. In the triangle ABC below, AB = AC and angle ADB = angle ADC.

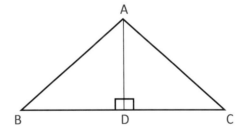

Prove that triangle ADB and triangle ADC are congruent.

(3 marks)

4. Work out the interior angle sum of an octagon.

(3 marks)

5. Solve the following equations.
   $i.\, 5y - 2 = 33 - 2y$

(2 marks)

   $ii.\, 2x - 3y = 5$
   $ 5x + 4y = 47$

(4 marks)

   $iii.\, x^2 - 11x + 24 = 0$

(3 marks)
(total 9 marks)

6. Ratios of $A:B = 4:3$ & $B:C = 9:10$.
   Work out the ratio of $A:C$. Give your answer in its simplest form.

(3 marks)

7. A & B are 2 events. Some probabilities are shown in the Venn diagram below.

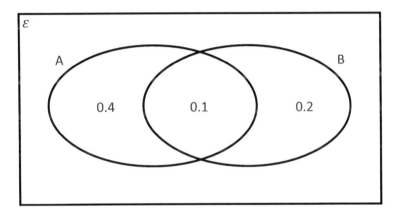

   Work out $P(A \cup B)'$

(2 marks)

8. Work out the value of $37^2 - 13^2$.

(3 marks)

9. Work out the exact value of

$$\left(\frac{125}{216}\right)^{-\frac{2}{3}}$$

(4 marks)

10. Anne, Beth & Chantelle shared £X in the ratio 2:5:6. Chantelle received £48 more than Anne.

i.   Find the value of X.

(3 marks)

ii.   How much did Beth receive?

(2 marks)
(total 5 marks)

11. Below are the first 4 terms of a quadratic sequence.

5,   14,   27,   44, ...

Work out an expression for the nth term of the sequence.

(4 marks)

12. The lines AB & RB are tangents to the circle at P & R respectively. O is the centre of the circle. The angle OPQ is 20° and sides PQ and PR are equal.

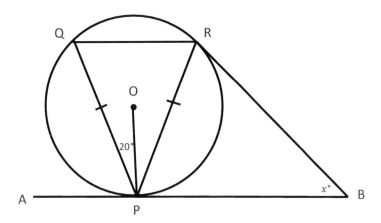

Work out the value of angle x.
(write reasons for each stage of your answer)

(4 marks)

13. Solve the following equation

$$\frac{9}{x-2} - \frac{10}{x} = 1$$

(5 marks)

14. Two solid cylinders A & B are mathematically similar.

Cylinder A has a height of $5cm$ and a volume of $20\pi cm^3$.
Cylinder B has a radius of $4cm$.

Work out the ratio of their lengths.

(4 marks)

15. Work out the equation of line AB, where $A(-2, 3)$ & $B(5, 17)$.

(4 marks)

16. a) Simplify fully

    i) $(\sqrt{3} - 1)(\sqrt{3} + 4)$

(2 marks)

    ii) $\sqrt{80} + \sqrt{45} - \sqrt{20}$

(2 marks)

b) Rationalise

i) $\frac{12}{\sqrt{3}}$

(2 marks)

    iii) $\frac{6+\sqrt{2}}{\sqrt{2}}$

(3 marks)

(total 9 marks)

17.

$$x^2 - 5x + 1 = (x - a)^2 + b$$

Work out the values of a & b.

(4 marks)

18. A quadratic graph intersects the x- axis at points $(-2, 0)$ & $(5, 0)$ and the y- axis at the point $(0, -10)$.

Work out the equation of the graph.

(4 marks)

19. Given that $\cos 30 = \frac{\sqrt{3}}{2}$, Work out the value of x.

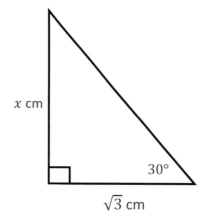

(3 marks)

Total for paper: 80 marks

End

GCSE Mathematics
Paper 2
(calculator)

Higher
Tier

Potential Paper B2

You must have: Ruler graduated in centimetres and millimetres, protractor, pair of compasses, pen, HB pencil, eraser.

Calculator is allowed

Time allowed
1 hour and 30minutes
Total 80 marks

Name

Date

1. Work out the area of the triangle below.

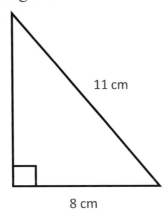

11 cm

8 cm

(4 marks)

2. Table shows marks achieved by students in a class.

Marks	Frequency (f)		
30-50	6		
50-60	8		
60-80	11		
80-90	4		
90-100	2		

Calculate an estimate for the mean mark.

(3 marks)

3. Work out the values of a & b.

$$3(4x + 5) + 2(3x + b) = ax + 11$$

(4 marks)

4. The radius of the circle below is 6cm and ABCD is a square.
    Calculate the area of the shaded region.

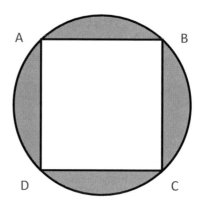

(5 marks)

5. A car accelerates from $5ms^{-1}$ to $20ms^{-1}$ in 6 seconds.
    Calculate the acceleration of the car.

(3 marks)

6. Work out

    i) $\dfrac{2.37^2 + 4.1 \times 2.3}{(6.1 - 5.35)}$ to 3 significant figures.

(3 marks)

    ii) $\dfrac{4.5 \times 10^8}{9 \times 10^{-3}}$ in standard form

(3 marks)
(total 6 marks)

7. The area of the triangle below is $6cm^2$.

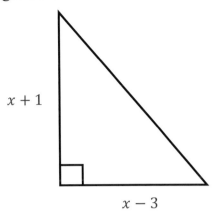

$x + 1$

$x - 3$

Work out the value of x.

(3 marks)

8. Tony sells boxes of 6 apples for £3.30 each and Kevin sells boxes of 5 apples for £2.80. Who is the better value for money?

(3 marks)

9. Density of gold is 20 g/cm^3.
   Calculate the mass of $200cm^3$ of gold.

(3 marks)

10. A cylinder has radius $3cm$ and height $6cm$. The cylinder is melted down and made into a sphere of radius ycm.

Calculate the value of y.

(4 marks)

11. Prove that the sum of any two odd integers is always even.

(4 marks)

12. A bag contains 12 sweets. 4 of them are red, 5 are blue and 3 are yellow. Molly picks 2 sweets at random.

Work out the probability of Molly picking 2 sweets of the same colour.

(4 marks)

13. Table below shows information about the heights of some plants.

Lengths(cm)	Frequency(f)	
2-5	4	
5-10	5	
10-13	6	
13-16	7	
16-20	2	

    i)   Represent the data above on a cumulative frequency graph in the grid below.

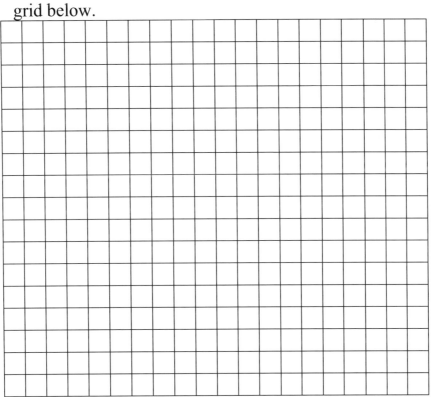

(3 marks)

    ii)   Work out the median height.

(2 marks)

    iii)   Work out the interquartile range.

(3 marks)
(total 8 marks)

14. A is directly proportional to B^2. When A is 45, B is -3.
   Work out the value of B, when A is 180.

(4 marks)

15. Factorise the following expressions fully.
   i) $4x^3 - 10x^2$

(2 marks)

   ii) $6x^2 - 13x + 6$

(3 marks)

   iii) $16x^2 - 9y^2$

(2 marks)
(total 7 marks)

16. The straight line L has the equation $3y - 12x = 30$.

   i)   Work out the gradient of L.

(2 marks)

   ii)   Write down the equation of perpendicular line to L through the origin.

(2 marks)
(total 4 marks)

17. A rectangle ABCD has points $A(-1,5), B(0,5), C(0,2)$ & $D(-1,2)$.
    i)   Plot the rectangle ABCD in the grid below.

(2 marks)

    ii)   Reflect ABCD in the line $x = 1$.

(3 marks)

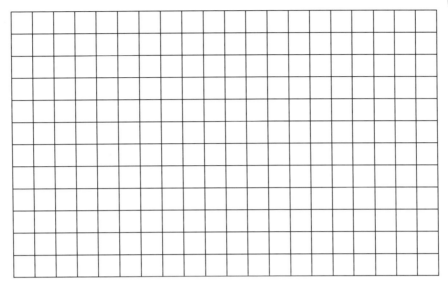

(total 5 marks)

18. O is the centre of the circle below. Angle SPR is 68°.
    Work out the angles SOR, PQS & PRS. Give reasons for each stage of your working.

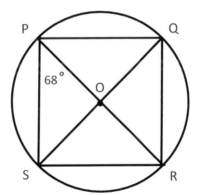

(4 marks)

Total for paper: 80 marks

End

GCSE Mathematics Paper 3 (calculator)

Higher Tier

Potential Paper B3

You must have: Ruler graduated in centimetres and millimetres, protractor, pair of compasses, pen, HB pencil, eraser.

Calculator is allowed

**Time allowed
1 hour and 30minutes
Total 80 marks**

Name

Date

1. Simplify fully

   i) $\dfrac{24x^2y^3 \times 35x^4y^9}{14x^5y^2 \times 18x^8y^5}$

   (3 marks)

   ii) $\left(\dfrac{2a^2}{3b^3}\right)^4$

   (2 marks)
   (total 5 marks)

2. A rectangle has length 14cm to the nearest centimetre and width 5.5cm to 1 decimal place.

   Calculate the lower bound for the area of the rectangle.

   (3 marks)

3. i) Work out the number of seconds in a day.

   (2 marks)

   ii) Write your answer to part (i) in standard form.

   (2 marks)
   (total 4 marks)

4. A curve C has equation $y = x^2 - 4x - 7$.
   Complete the table below and plot the curve C for x −values −2 to 6 on the space provided below.

x	-2	-1	0	1	2	3	4	5	6
y									

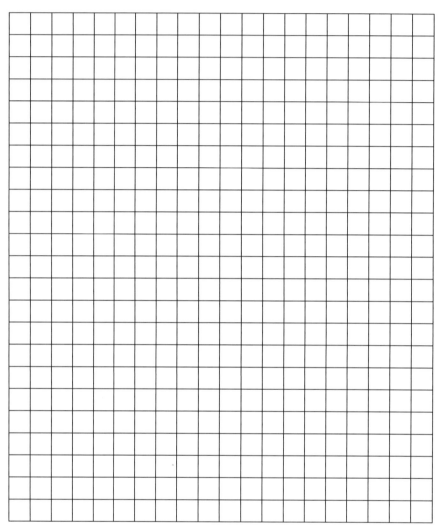

(4 marks)

5. Each interior angle of an n-sided regular polygon is 165°.
   Work out the value of n.

(3 marks)

6. A room is 10m by 6m. It is to be tiled using tiles 60cm by 20cm costing 12 pence each. Calculate the cost of tiles required to cover the entire floor area of the room.

(4 marks)

7. Plot the triangle ABC where $A(3,1), B(5,7)$ & $C(3,7)$ and enlarge the triangle ABC by a scale factor of 2 about the point (1,1) in the grind below.

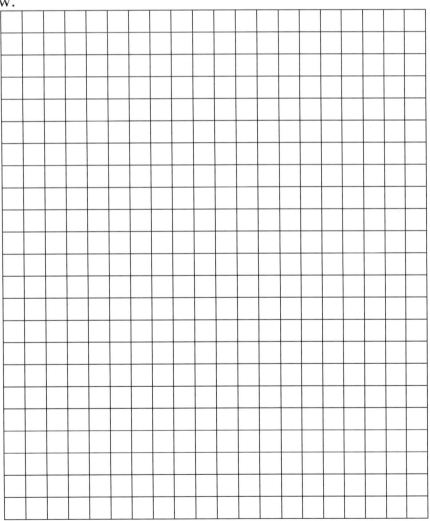

(3 marks)

8. i) Solve the following simultaneous equations

$5x - 2y = 8$

$3x - 7y = -1$

(4 marks)

ii) Simplify fully

$$\frac{2x^2 - 6x}{x^2 - 5x + 6}$$

(3 marks)

(total 7 marks)

9. A bag has 4 mangos and 3 apples. John eats 2 fruits at random.

    i)   Draw a tree diagram showing all possible outcomes.

(3 marks)

    ii)   Work out the probability of John eating at least 1 apple.

(2 marks)

(total 5 marks)

10. A car has a speed of $20ms^{-1}$ & a van has a speed of $75kmh^{-1}$.
    Which vehicle is moving faster?

(3 marks)

11. A, B & C shared £y in the ratio $7 : 5 : 9$.
    A has £130 more than B.
    Work out the value of y.

(3 marks)

12. Prove algebraically that the multiple of any two integers which are
    divisible and 2 and 3 respectively is also a multiple of 6.

(3 marks)

13. Solve the following equation by completing the square and round your answers to 2 decimal places.

$$x^2 - 6x + 1 = 0$$

(5 marks)

14. Sketch the graph of $y = \cos x$ for $0 \leq x \leq 360°$.

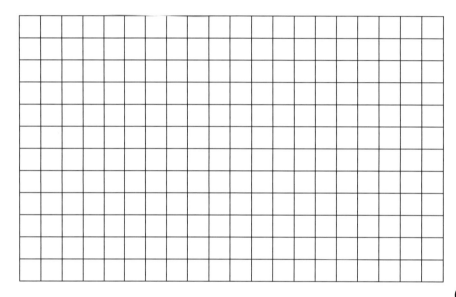

(3 marks)

15. Expand and simplify fully

$$(3x - 1)^2 - (4x + 3)(2x - 5)$$

(4 marks)

16. Work out the area of the shape PQRS.

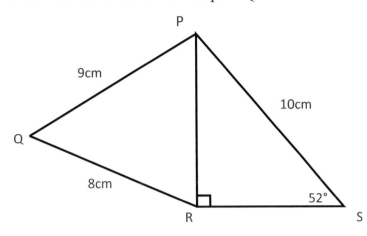

(6 marks)

17. $x^3 - 3x^2 + 1 = 0$

    i)   Show that the above equation can be rearranged to give
$$x = \sqrt[3]{3x^2 - 1}$$

(2 marks)

    ii)   Using the iterative formula below,
$$x_{n+1} = \sqrt[3]{3x_n^2 - 1}, \, x_0 = 3.$$
Calculate to 4 decimal places the values of x_1 & x_2.

(2 marks)
(total 4 marks)

18. Marks achieved by students in a class is given below.

Marks	Frequency (f)		
20-50	6		
50-70	12		
70-80	10		
80-95	6		
95-100	2		

Draw a histogram to represent the above data.

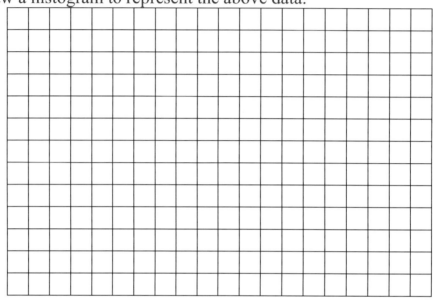

(3 marks)

19. The diagram below shows the vectors $\overrightarrow{OA} = a$ & $\overrightarrow{OB} = b$.
    D is the midpoint of OA and the ratio $AC: CB = 3: 2$.

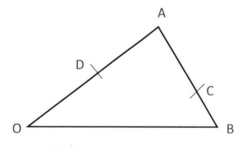

Work out $\overrightarrow{DC}$.

(4 marks)

20. A solid cone has radius 6cm & height 8cm. A solid cylinder with the same surface area as the cone above has a height of 4cm.

Work out the radius of the cylinder.

(4 marks)

Total for paper: 80 marks

End

Section C

GCSE Mathematics
Paper 1
(non-calculator)

Higher
Tier

Potential Paper C1

You must have: Ruler graduated in centimetres and millimetres, protractor, pair of compasses, pen, HB pencil, eraser.

Calculator is not allowed

Time allowed
1 hour and 30minutes
Total 80 marks

Name

Date

1. Simplify fully

$$(3a^5b^3)^3$$

(3 marks)

2. $a = 2, b = -1, c = -3$
   Work out the following

   i)　　$5a - 3b$

(2 marks)

   ii)　　$a^2 - b^2 + c^2$

(2 marks)
(total 4 marks)

3. Johannes had £300. He gave $\frac{1}{5}$ to his brother and gave the rest to his mother and father in the ratio 3:5. Work out the amount received by his father.

(4 marks)

4. A cuboid has length 8 cm, width 5 cm and height h cm. The volume of the cuboid is $80\ cm^3$.

   Work out the surface area of the cuboid.

   (4 marks)

5. Garry ran 120m in 20 seconds.
   i)   Calculate his speed in m/s

   (1 mark)

   ii)   Convert his speed to km/h

   (3marks)
   (total 4 marks)

6. Solve the following simultaneous equations algebraically

$$xy = 6$$
$$y - x = 1$$

(5 marks)

7. Find highest common factor (HCF) and lowest common multiple (LCM) of 84 & 105.

(4 marks)

8. (a) Write down the exact value of sin 30

(1 mark)

(b) Here is a right-angled triangle ABC where AB = BC

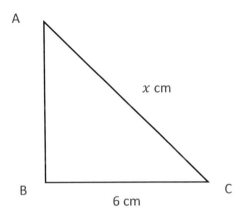

Given that, $sin45 = \frac{1}{\sqrt{2}}$

Work out the value of x.

(3 marks)
(total 4 marks)

9. The below shows some data for marks achieved by 30 students.

Marks	Frequency (f)	
40-50	3	
50-60	8	
60-70	10	
70-90	7	
90-100	2	

Draw a frequency polygon for the marks.

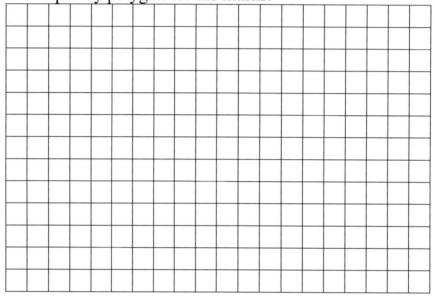

(3 marks)-35

10. (a) Simplify fully

$$\frac{4x^2 - 9}{2x^2 + 5x + 3}$$

(3 marks)

(b) Factorise fully

$$4a^2 - ab - 3b^2$$

(2 marks)
(total 5 marks)

11. Work out the following and write the answer as a mixed fraction if appropriate.

$$4\frac{3}{4} \div (3\frac{2}{3} - 1\frac{1}{2})$$

(4 marks)

12. Angle BCD in the diagram below is 128° and O is the centre of the circle.

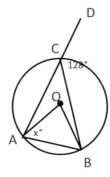

Find x? (write reasons for each stage of your working)

(4 marks)

13. (a) Plot the triangle ABC where A (1,1), B (1,5) & C (4,1) on the grid below.

(1 mark)

(b) Translate the triangle ABC by vector

$$\begin{pmatrix} 1 \\ -7 \end{pmatrix}$$

(2 marks)
(total 3 marks)

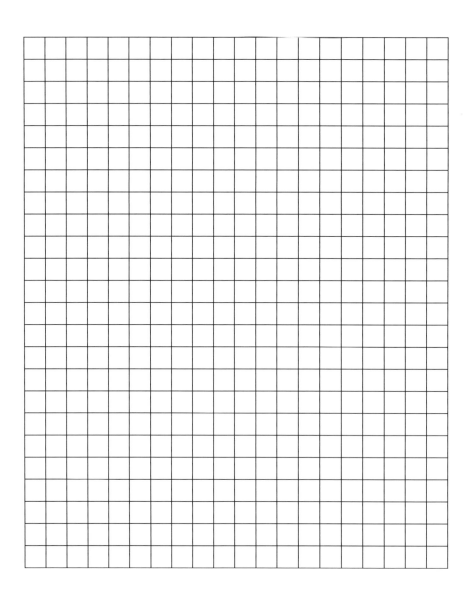

(total 3 marks)

14. (a) Work out the value of

$$\left(\frac{27}{125}\right)^{\frac{2}{3}}$$

(2 marks)

(b) $3^{x+1} \times 9^x = 3^{2x+5}$, find the value of x?

(3 marks)

(total 5 marks)

15. A sphere has radius of $6cm$ and a cylinder has radius $3cm$. Volumes of the sphere and the cylinder are equal.

i) Work out the volume of the sphere in terms of π.

(2 marks)

ii) Work out the height of the cylinder?

(3 marks)

(total 5 marks)

16. Write the following as fractions

    i)   0.3

                                                        (1 mark)

    ii) $0.\dot{3}$

                                                        (2 marks)

    iii) $0.0\dot{3}$

                                                        (2 marks)

    iv) $0.\dot{1}\dot{3}$

                                                        (3 marks)
                                               (total 8 marks)

17. $x^2 - 10x + 3 = (x - a)^2 + b$, where a & b are integers.
    Find the values of a & b.

                                                        (3 marks)

18. Plot the graph of $y = x^2 - 2x - 3$ in the space below for values of $-2 \leq x \leq 4$.

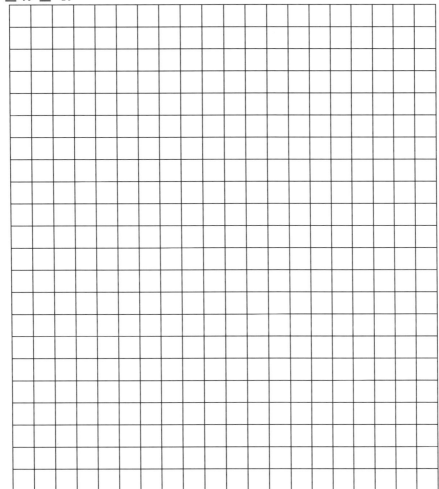

(4 marks)

19. $f(x) = (2x + 1)^2$, $g(x) = 3x - 2$

Show that $fg(x) = 9(2x - 1)^2$

(4 marks)

Total for paper: 80 marks

End

GCSE Mathematics Paper 2 (calculator)

Higher Tier

Potential Paper C2

You must have: Ruler graduated in centimetres and millimetres, protractor, pair of compasses, pen, HB pencil, eraser.

Calculator is allowed

Time allowed
1 hour and 30minutes
Total 80 marks

Name

Date

1. Solve the following inequalities
   i) $2x - 1 \geq 3 - 6x$

(2 marks)

   ii) $x^2 - 3x - 4 < 0$

(3 marks)
(total 5 marks)

2. Lines AC & PS are parallel.

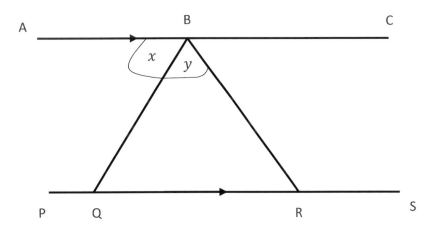

Show that $B\hat{R}S = x + y$
(write reasons for each stage of your working)

(3 marks)

3. A house is £250,000. It increases in value by 6% every year. Work out its value in 8 years?

(3 marks)

4. A sports hall is 60m long and 20m wide. The hall is to be tiled with tiles which are 60cm long and 15cm wide. Each tile costs 45p. Calculate the cost of tiles required to cover the entire sports hall.

(4 marks)

5. Work out the following
$$\frac{(2.5 \times 10^{-3}) \times (1.3 \times 10^{8})}{(6.5 \times 10^{2})}$$
Write your answer in standard form.

(3 marks)

6. $A(2,5)$ & $B(4,15)$
  i) Work out the midpoint of AB

(2 marks)

  ii) Work out the equation of the line AB

(3 marks)

(total 5 marks)

7. A rectangle has vertices $A(-1,3), B(-1,-1), C(2,3), D(2,-1)$
  i) Plot the rectangle in the space below
    (1 mark)
  ii) Rotate the rectangle above 90° clockwise about $(-2,0)$
    (3 marks)

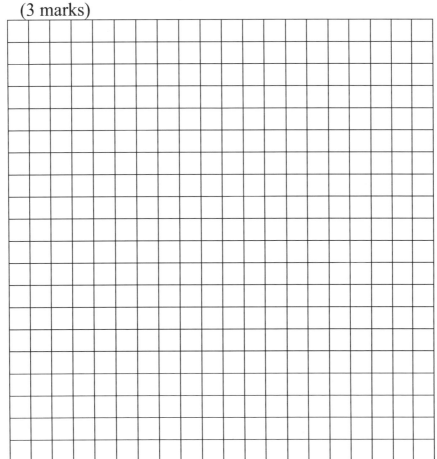

(total 4 marks)

8. Work out area of the triangle ABC.

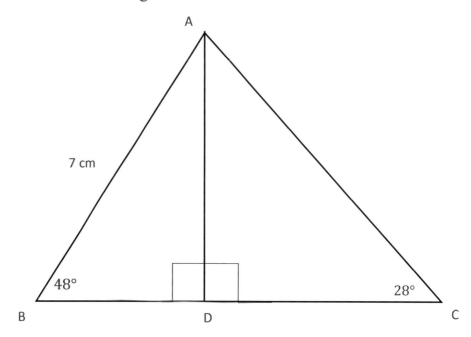

9. There are 6 red sweets and 4 blue sweets in a packet. Tom picks 2 sweets one after the other.

    i)   Draw a tree diagram for all possible outcomes.

(3 marks)

    ii)   Work out the probability of Tom eating at least 1 blue sweet.

(3 marks)
(total 6 marks)

10. The table below shows the heights of 40 people.

Height(cm)	Frequency(f)	
120-150	7	
150-160	10	
160-170	12	
170-190	8	
190-200	3	

i)   Draw a cumulative frequency curve for above data

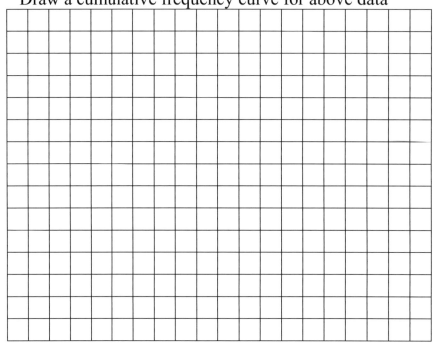

(2 marks)

ii)   Work out the median and interquartile range.

(4 marks)

iii)   Calculate the percentage of people over 180cm.

(2 marks)
(total 8 marks)

11. Sector AOB is shown below where length AB is 10cm.
    a) work out the radius of sector AOB where distance AB is 10cm.

(2 marks)

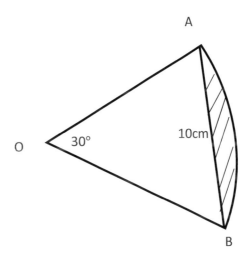

b) Calculate the area of shaded region.

(3 marks)
(total 5 marks)

12. a) Express following as a single fraction in the simplest form.

$$\frac{4}{x-1} - \frac{1}{x-2}$$

(3 marks)

b) hence or otherwise, solve the equation

$$\frac{4}{x-1} - \frac{1}{x-2} = 1$$

(3 marks)

(total 6 marks)

13. A trapezium ABCD has parallel sides AB and CD, where AB = 4cm and CD = 10cm. A square has length 6cm.

Area of the square is 75% of area of the trapezium. Work out the height of the trapezium.

(4 marks)

14. Make x the subject.

$$y = \frac{3x + 2}{2x - 1}$$

(3 marks)

15. O is the centre of the circle drawn below. Lines AB & AC are tangents to the circle at points B & C respectively. Angle ACB is 48°.

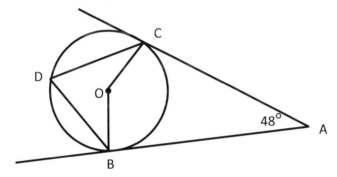

Work out the BDC. (give reasons for each stage of your working)

(5 marks)

16. A, B& C shared £X in ratio 5:3:7.

C received £120 more than B. Find the value X.

(4 marks)

17. Work out the area of triangle PQR drawn below.

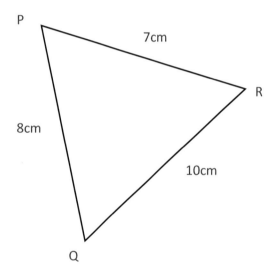

(4 marks)

18. $\overrightarrow{OA} = a, \overrightarrow{OB} = b, C$ is such that $AC : CB = 2 : 1. D$ is the midpoint of OA.
Work out $\overrightarrow{DC}$.

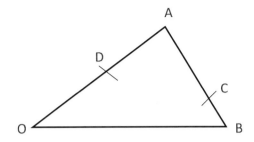

(4 marks)

Total for paper: 80 marks

End

GCSE Mathematics Paper 3 (calculator)

Higher Tier

Potential Paper C3

You must have: Ruler graduated in centimetres and millimetres, protractor, pair of compasses, pen, HB pencil, eraser.

Calculator is allowed

**Time allowed
1 hour and 30minutes
Total 80 marks**

Name

Date

1. A = 5500 (correct to 2 significant figures)
   B = 20.5 (correct to 1 decimal place)

   Write down upper and lower bounds for A & B.

   (3 marks)

2. A computer is £559 after a 35% discount. Work out the price before discount.

   (3 marks)

3. A set of data for lengths are tabled below.

Length (m)	Frequency		
10-20	3		
20-40	4		
40-50	7		
50-80	9		
80-100	2		

   Represent data on a histogram in the grind.

   (4 marks)

4. An interior angle of a regular polygon is 162°. Work out the number of sides of this polygon.

(3 marks)

5. Find x in each triangle below.

i)

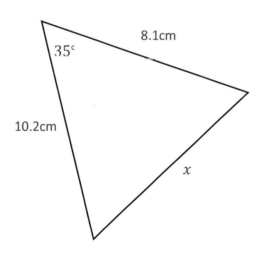

8.1cm

35ᶜ

10.2cm

x

(3 marks)

ii)

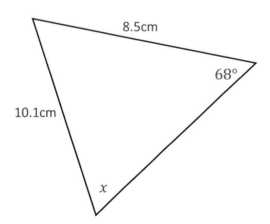

8.5cm

68°

10.1cm

x

(3 marks)
(total 6 marks)

6. A solid cylinder is made from metal. It has a radius 6cm and a height 12cm. The cylinder is melted down and made into a sphere.

   Work out the radius of the sphere?

   (5marks)

7. Expand and simplify
   i) $(x - 3)(2x + 1)(3x - 2)$

   (3 marks)

   ii) $(2x - 1)^2 - (3x + 1)(x - 4)$

   (3 marks)
   (total 6 marks)

8. Andy invested £3500 in a bank. The bank offers 5.5% compound interest for first 2 years and 4% compound interest after that.
   Work out his balance after 5 years.

(3 marks)

9. Sketch the graph of $y = \cos x$ for $0 \leq x \leq 360$ in the space below.

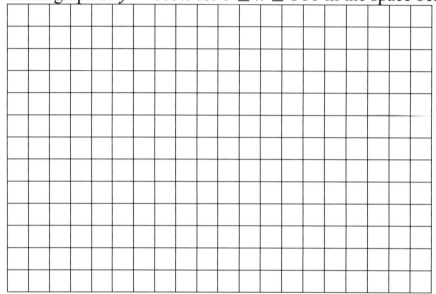

(2 marks)

10. A solid cone has a radius of 5 cm and a vertical height of 12cm.
    i)   Calculate the volume of cone to 2 decimals.

(2 marks)

    ii)   Calculate the surface area of the cone to 2 decimals.

(4 marks)
(total 6 marks)

11. $x^3 - 5x + 1 = 0$

    i)   Show that above equation has a solution between $x = 2$ & $x = 3$.

(2 marks)

    ii)   Show that the equation can be rearranged to give
$$x = \sqrt[3]{5x - 1}$$

(1 marks)

    iii)   Starting with $x_0 = 2$, use the iteration formula below 3 times to find an estimate for the solution to $x^3 - 5x + 1 = 0$

$$x_{n+1} = \sqrt[3]{5x_n - 1}$$

(3 marks)
(total 6 marks)

12. A is proportional to B^2. When $A = 75, B = 5$.

    i)   Find A, when $B = 2$.

(3 marks)

    ii)   Find B, when $A = 147$.

(3 marks)
(total 6 marks)

13. Prove algebraically that the difference between any odd number and any even number is always odd.

(3 marks)

14. Work out the area of shaded region.

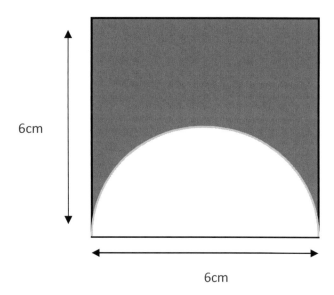

6cm

6cm

(4 marks)

15. Liquid X has density 2 g/cm^3
    Liquid Y has density 5 g/cm^3
    300ml of liquid X is mixed with 200ml of liquid Y.
    Work out the density of the mixture.

(4 marks)

16. Calculate the distance BD.

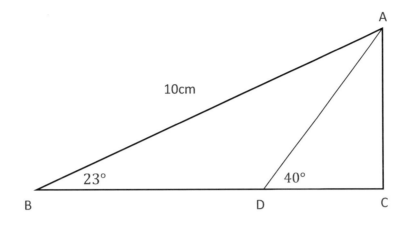

(4 marks)

17. Here are the first 4 terms of a quadratic sequence.

$$-1, \quad 3, \quad 13, \quad 29$$

Work out an expression for the nth term of the sequence.

(4 marks)

18. Solve algebraically the simultaneous equations
$$x^2 + y^2 = 58$$
$$2x - y = 11$$

(5 marks)

19. Work out the equation of perpendicular line to AB through point $(0, 3)$, where $A(2, 7)$ & $B(6, 1)$.

(3 marks)

Total for paper: 80 marks

End

Section D

GCSE Mathematics
Paper 1
(non-calculator)

Higher
Tier

Potential Paper D1

You must have: Ruler graduated in centimetres and millimetres, protractor, pair of compasses, pen, HB pencil, eraser.

Calculator is not allowed

Time allowed
1 hour and 30minutes
Total 80 marks

Name

Date

1. (a) Write 48 as a product of its prime factors.

(2 marks)

(b) Find highest common factor and lowest common multiple of 48 & 72

(3 marks)

(total 5 marks)

2. Anne, Bryan and Charlie shared n sweets in ratio 3:5:9. Charlie had 30 sweets more than Anne. Find the total number of sweets n?

(4 marks)

3. AC is a diameter of the circle with centre O drawn below. Angle OBA is 33°. ED is a tangent to circle at C.

   Show that angle BCD is 33°. (give a reason for each stage)

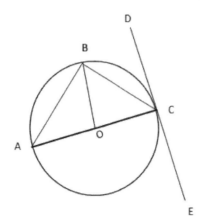

(4 marks)

4. A rectangle has length 35.5cm and perimeter 85.2cm. What percentage of length is the width of this rectangle?

Perimeter 85.2cm

35.5cm

(4 marks)

5. (i) Work out 2.32×1.413

(2 marks)

(ii) Estimate the following

$$\frac{49.83 \times 3.99}{\sqrt{4.81} + 20.45}$$

(2 marks)

(total 4 marks)

6. Show that area of Δ ABC is $54cm^2$.

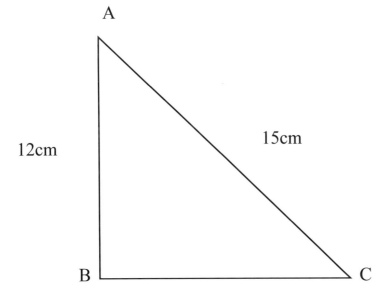

(4 marks)

7. Plot $y = x^2 + 2x - 5$ for $-5 \leq x \leq 3$

(4 marks)

8. Write the following in ascending order if $x > 1$

$$x^{3/2} \ , \ -x^2 \ , \ x^0 , \ x^{2/3} \ , (-x)^2$$

(3 marks)

9. Convert the following into m^3

(i) $200cm^3$

(ii) $2km^3$

(4 marks)

10. Work out the following

(i) $8^{\frac{1}{3}}$

(1 mark)

(ii) $\left(\frac{125}{216}\right)^{\frac{2}{3}}$

(3 marks)

(total 4 marks)

11. Solve the following

$2a - 3b = 5$

$5a + 4b = 47$

(4 marks)

12. The table shows information about weights in Kilograms of a group of sixth form students.

Weight (Kg)	Frequency (f)
40-50	7
50-60	11
60-70	9
70-100	5

(i)   Write down the modal weight class?

(1 mark)

(ii)   Work out the median weight class?

(2 marks)

(iii)   Draw a frequency polygon for this information

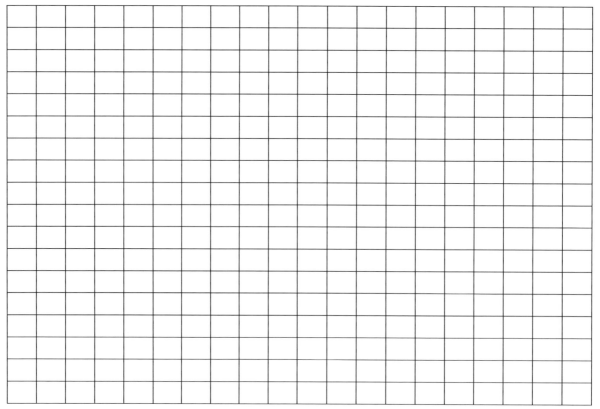

(3 marks)

(total 6 marks)

13. A is directly proportional to B. When A is 30, B is 6.

(i)   Find A when B is 9?

(3 marks)

(ii)   Find B when A is 135?

(2 marks)

(total 5 marks)

14. Andy is (x) years old and Brian is (y) years old. The ratio of their ages now is 3:5.

In 10 years, the ratio of their ages will be 5:7. Find x and y?

(5 marks)

15. $x = 0.2\dot{7}$, Prove algebraically that $x = \frac{5}{18}$

(3 marks)

16. Joseph had n sweets. He gave 30% of them to his sister and $\frac{1}{5}$ of them to his parents. From the rest, he ate 20% of them. He now has 36 sweets left. Work out the value n?

(5 marks)

17. Prove algebraically that any two odd numbers always add up to an even number?

(4 marks)

18. Coordinates of two points are given by A (2,3) B (6,10).

(i) Find the midpoint of line AB.

(1 mark)

(ii) Find the equation of perpendicular line to AB through the midpoint of AB.

(4 marks)

(Total 5 marks)

19. Show that $\dfrac{1+ \sqrt{2}}{3- \sqrt{2}} = \dfrac{a+ b\sqrt{2}}{7}$

Where a and b are integers.

(3marks)

Total for paper: 80 marks

End

GCSE Mathematics
Paper 2
(calculator)

Higher
Tier

Potential Paper D2

You must have: Ruler graduated in centimetres and millimetres, protractor, pair of compasses, pen, HB pencil, eraser.

Calculator is allowed

Time allowed
1 hour and 30minutes
Total 80 marks

Name

Date

1. Solve the following equations.

(i) $3(5x - 1) + 2(3x - 7) = 5(3x + 11)$

(3 marks)

(ii) $2x^2 - 5x - 12 = 0$

(3 marks)

(total 6 marks)

2. A house is worth £250,000 this year and the value of the house increases by 7% each year. What will the house be worth in 3 years' time?

(3marks)

3. The perimeter of the rectangle drawn below is 200% of the perimeter of the equilateral triangle drawn below. Calculate the length of a side of the equilateral triangle. (to one decimal place)

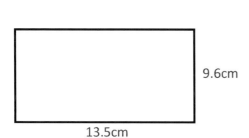

9.6cm

13.5cm

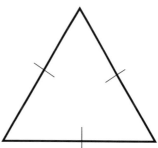

(3marks)

4. There are 6 yellow sweets and 4 red sweets in a bag. Jo and Ben eat a sweet each.

   Calculate the probability of at least one of them eating a red sweet?

   (3 marks)

5. A triangle ABC has vertices A (1,2), B (4,2), C (1,6).
   (i)   Plot the triangle ABC on the grid below

   (1 mark)

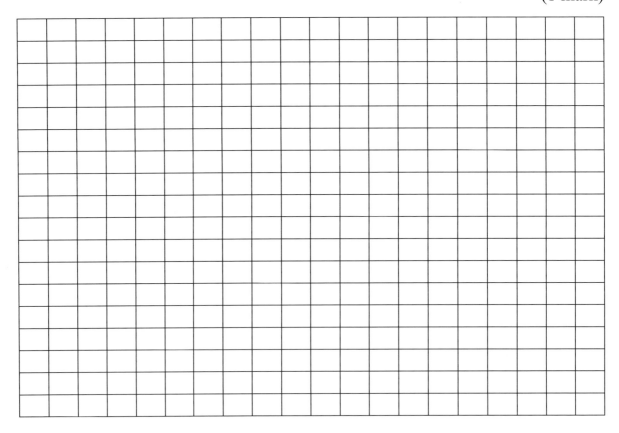

   (ii)   Translate the triangle ABC by vector $\begin{pmatrix} -3 \\ -1 \end{pmatrix}$.

   (2 marks)

   (total 3 marks)

6. (a) $y^x \times y^{2x+1} = y^7$ Find x?

(2 marks)

(b) Simplify $(2a^3b^{-2})^3$

(2 marks)

(c) Work out $\left(\dfrac{27}{64}\right)^{-\frac{4}{3}}$

(2 marks)

(total 6 marks)

7. Calculate the angle ADC to one decimal place?

   Where AB = 14cm, BC = 10cm & AD = 16cm.

   Angles ACB & ACD are right angles.

(write your answer to one decimal place)

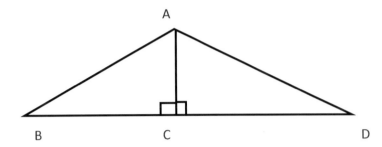

(4 marks)

8. A = 1200cm (correct to 3 significant figures)
   B = 500cm (correct to 1 significant figure)

   Calculate limits of accuracy for $\dfrac{A}{B}$.

(4 marks)

9. A rectangular canteen is 40m long and 20m wide. It is to be tiled using rectangular tiles which are 50cm by 40cm. Each tile costs 68pence and the builder charges £65 per $100m^2$ of tiling.

Calculate the total cost of tiling?

(5 marks)

10. John flew an aeroplane on a bearing of 075° from A to B at a speed of 240km per hour for 45 minutes. He then flew on a bearing of 180° from B to C for 1 hour and 20 minutes.

Calculate the distance from A to C on a straight line. (write your answer to 3 significant figures)

(5 marks)

11. Marks for a year 11 maths examination is given in the table below.

Marks %	Frequency		
40-50	7		
50-70	18		
70-80	12		
80-90	6		
90-100	2		

Calculate the mean mark? (write your answer to nearest integer)

(2 marks)

12. How many sides does the regular polygon B have?

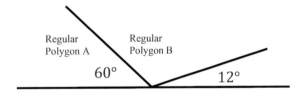

(2 marks)

13. John wants to invest £15,000 for 4 years. Two banks have the following offers available.

Bank A	Bank B
8% for first year 2% per annum compound interest thereafter	4.5% per year compound interest

Which bank is more profitable for John?

(show clear working)

(4 marks)

14. Solve the following inequalities.
(i) $3(2x - 1) < 2(x + 7)$

(2 marks)

(ii) $x^2 - 2x - 15 > 0$

(3 marks)

(total 5 marks)

15. Six different coloured balls are in a box. Two balls are picked at random. How many different combinations are possible?

(2 marks)

16. Solve $x^2 - 16x + 17 = 0$ using completing the square method.
(write your answer to 3 significant figures)

(3 marks)

17. Salaries of a company are given in the table below.

Salaries (£)	Frequency	
1000-2000	12	
2000-4000	17	
4000-7000	8	
7000-9000	5	
9000-10000	2	

(i)   Draw a cumulative frequency graph on the grid

(2 marks)

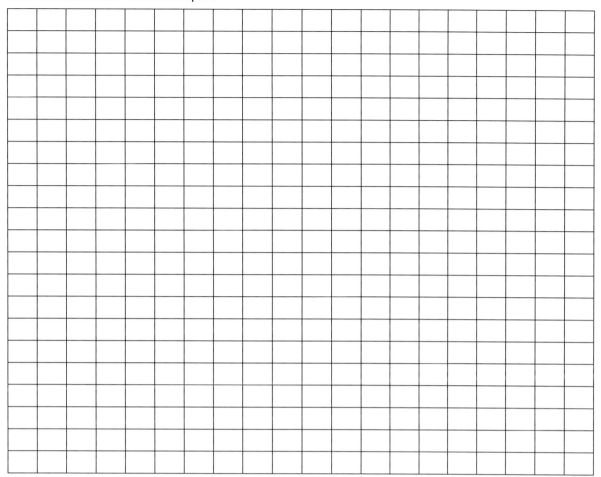

(ii)   Work out the median salary

(1 mark)

(iii)   Work out the interquartile range

(3 marks)

(total 6 marks)

18. The coordinates of points P, Q, R are (-4, 2), (3, 9) and (2, 4) respectively. The line PQ meets x-axis at A and the line PR meets y-axis at B. Calculate the distance AB.

(6 marks)

19. The functions f and g are such that

$$f(x) = 3x + 1 \text{ and } g(x) = 2x - 3$$

Work out $f^{-1}(x)$, $fg(x)$ and $gf(3)$

(4 marks)

20. Calculate the area of the segment AB.

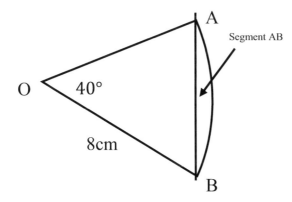

(4 marks)

Total for paper: 80 marks

End

GCSE Mathematics
Paper 3
(calculator)

Higher
Tier

Potential Paper D3

You must have: Ruler graduated in centimetres and millimetres, protractor, pair of compasses, pen, HB pencil, eraser.

Calculator is allowed

**Time allowed
1 hour and 30minutes
Total 80 marks**

Name

Date

1. Draw a histogram for the information given in the table.

Lengths (cm)	Frequency		
40-70	6		
70-80	4		
80-90	5		
90-150	12		

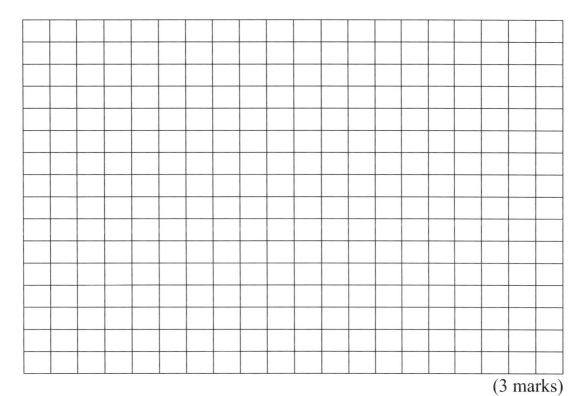

(3 marks)

2. Mrs. Smith bought 2 bags of onions for £1.37 each, 3kg of potatoes for £1.74 each and a whole chicken for £5.99. She received a loyalty discount of 16% from the shop.
Calculate her total cost after discount?

(3 marks)

3. Andy drove 48km in 45 minutes from A to B. He then drove 120km in 2 hours and 30 minutes from B to C.
   Calculate his average speed from A to C?

   (3 marks)

4. Thomas is 2 years older than Ashley and Ashley is twice the age of Max. Their total age is 47 years.
   How many years is Thomas older than Max?

   (3 marks)

5. A (1,6), B (3, -10)
   (i)   Work out the midpoint of AB

   (1 mark)

   (ii)   Find the equation of perpendicular line to AB through its midpoint.

   (4 marks)

   (total 5 marks)

6. Perimeter of the rectangle is equal to the circumference of the circle drawn below. Calculate the area of the circle.

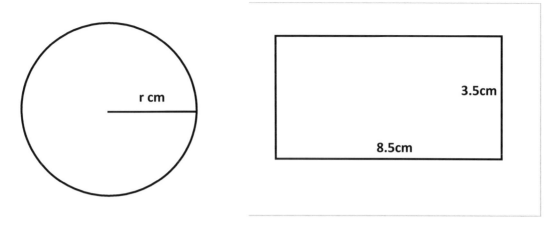

(4 marks)

7. The table below shows number of people who achieved grades 7, 8 and 9 in three subjects in an examination.

	Mathematics	English	Science
Grade 9	2	7	4
Grade 8	6	7	5
Grade 7	15	38	21

a) Jacob wants to pick a sample of 30 people for a survey. How many science students should he pick?

(2 marks)

b) A county had 25,000 students taking these three subjects in an examination.
Estimate the number of people we can expect to achieve grade 9 in mathematics.

(3 marks)
(total 5 marks)

8. Work out the following and write your answer as an ordinary number.

$$\frac{(5.6 \times 10^5) \times (2 \times 10^{-3})}{7.4 \times 10^3}$$

(3 marks)

9. A laptop is worth £950 brand new. It would lose value by 27% each year. Sarah says in 7 years' time the laptop will be worth less than £100. Is Sarah correct? (show clear working)

(3 marks)

10. Company A makes 70% of cars in a country and company B makes the rest of cars in the same country. A car from company A has a 4% chance of a breakdown and a car from company B has a 1% chance of a breakdown. Steven bought a car.
Calculate the probability of a breakdown?

(3 marks)

11. Factorise the following expressions fully.

(i) $3x^2 - 12x$

(1 mark)

(ii) $14a^2 + 8a$

(1 mark)

(iii) $y^2 - 100$

(1 mark)

(iv) $4a^2 - 9$

(2 marks)

(v) $x^2 - 7x - 30$

(2 marks)

(vi) $3x^2 - 13x - 10$

(3marks)

(total 10 marks)

12. Cylinder A has a radius r cm and height h cm.
Cylinder B has a radius 4 cm and height 10 cm.
They are mathematically similar.

Show that the volume of cylinder A is $\frac{4}{25}\pi h^3$ cm^3

(4marks)

13. Ben plays a game twice. He has a 0.5 chance of winning the first time. If he wins the game first time, then he has a 0.75 chance of winning the game second time around. If he loses the first time, then the chance of him winning the second time is 0.4.

(i)   Draw a tree diagram showing all probabilities.

(3 marks)

(ii)   Calculate the probability of winning only one of the games.

(2 marks)

(iii)   Calculate the probability of winning at least one game.

(2 marks)

(total 7 marks)

14. Using a right-angled isosceles triangle,
    show that tan 45 = 1

(3 marks)

15. Solve $3x^2 - 5x - 7 = 0$
    (write your answers to 2 decimal places)

(3 marks)

16. A liquid has density $4g/cm^3$ correct to 1 significant figure. A sample of this liquid is 150ml to nearest millilitre.

Calculate the minimum possible mass of this sample.

(4 marks)

17. PR $= 7\ cm$, PS $= 10\ cm$, angle PSR $= 38°$ and area of triangle PQR is $35cm^2$.

Calculate the area of triangle PQS. (show clear steps with working)

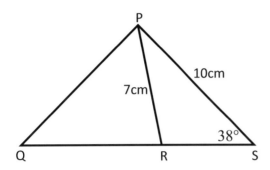

(5 marks)

18. Vectors $\overrightarrow{OA} = a$ and $\overrightarrow{OB} = b$. Point C is such that ratio BC:CA $= 3:2$.

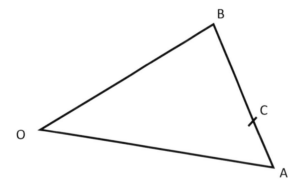

Work out the following in terms a and b

(i) $\overrightarrow{AB}$ (2 marks)   (ii) $\overrightarrow{AC}$ (2 marks)

(total 4 marks)

19.(i) Plot $y = x^2 - 2x - 5$ and $y = 2x - 1$ for $-3 \leq x \leq 5$.

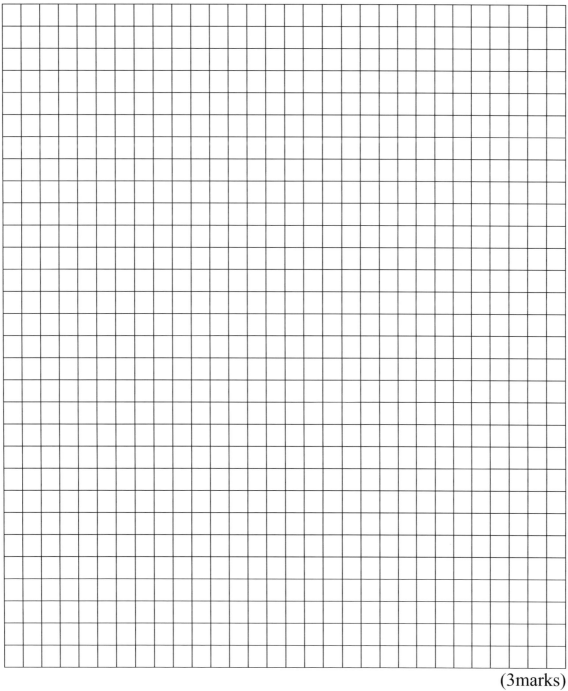

(3marks)

(ii) Using your graphs, solve the simultaneous equations.

$y = x^2 - 2x - 5$

$y = 2x - 1$

(2marks)

(total 5 marks)

Total for paper: 80 marks

End

Section E

GCSE Mathematics Paper 1 (non-calculator)

Higher Tier

Potential Paper E1

You must have: Ruler graduated in centimetres and millimetres, protractor, pair of compasses, pen, HB pencil, eraser.

Calculator is not allowed

Time allowed
1 hour and 30minutes
Total 80 marks

Name

Date

1. Work out $3\frac{2}{3} - (4\frac{1}{2} \div 2\frac{1}{4})$

(3 marks)

2. First three terms of a sequence are 13, 17, 21, ….
    (i)   Find n^{th} term of the sequence

(1 mark)

   (ii)   Find 75th term

(1 mark)

   (iii)   Is 119 a term in the sequence? (show clear working)

(2 marks)

(total 4 marks)

3. James invested £5000 in a bank account for 3 years. The bank offers 4% simple interest per annum.
   Calculate his account balance at the end of 3 years.

(3 marks)

4. In an online competition, a prize is won by a contestant every 17 minutes. Estimate how many prizes are won in a month.

(3 marks)

5. Calculate the area of triangle ABC.

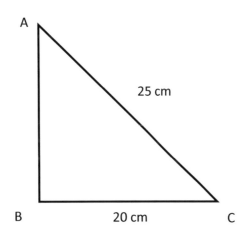

(3 marks)

6. Three coordinates A, B, C are as follows A (2, -2), B (4, 1) & C (6, 5)
(i) Work out the midpoint of AB

(1 mark)

(ii) Work out gradient of AB

(1 mark)

(iii) Find the equation of the line through midpoint of AB and parallel to BC.

(3 marks)

(total 5 marks)

7. A line segment AB is drawn below.
   The point C is such that the angle BAC is 60°. Construct the line AC.

A ———————————————————————————— B

(3 marks)

8. Find the volume of a cylinder whose radius is 6cm and the height 15cm.
   (write your answer in terms of π)

(2 marks)

9. Work out the following

(i) $125^{\frac{2}{3}}$

(2marks)

(ii) $(\frac{2}{7})^0$

(1mark)

(iii) $(\frac{32}{243})^{-\frac{3}{5}}$

(3 marks)

(total 6 marks)

10. A, B & C shared £240 in ratio 3:x:5.

    A received £40 less than C. Find x.

(3 marks)

11. AD and CD are tangents to the circle at A and C respectively. O is the centre of the circle. Angle ADC is 38°.

    Work out the angle ABC. (give reasons for each stage)

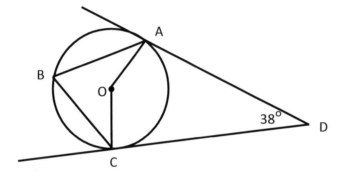

(4 marks)

12. Prove that if a number is a multiple of 2 and a multiple of 3, then it is also a multiple of 6.

(3 marks)

13. Show that $\left(7 - \sqrt{5} \right)\left(5 + \sqrt{5} \right) = a\left(b + \sqrt{5} \right)$

Where a *and* b are integers. Find a & b.

(3 marks)

14. A is inversely proportional to B. When A = 2, B= 6.
    Find B when A = 48.

(3 marks)

15. Factorise fully

(i) $2x^3 - 6x^2 - 8x$

(2 marks)

(ii) $x^3 - x$

(2 marks)

(total 4 marks)

16. Probability of Simon attending school late on any day is 0.15.
What is the probability of Simon attending school on time at least one day out of two consecutive days?

(4 marks)

17. Simplify $\dfrac{2}{2x-3} + \dfrac{3}{5x+3}$

(3 marks)

18. Below is a sketch of y = f(x) where A (-1, 0), B (2, -3), C (5, 0) are three points on the curve.

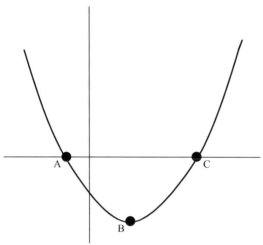

Sketch on the same axes below

(i)   y = f (x – 3) and (ii) y = 3f(x)

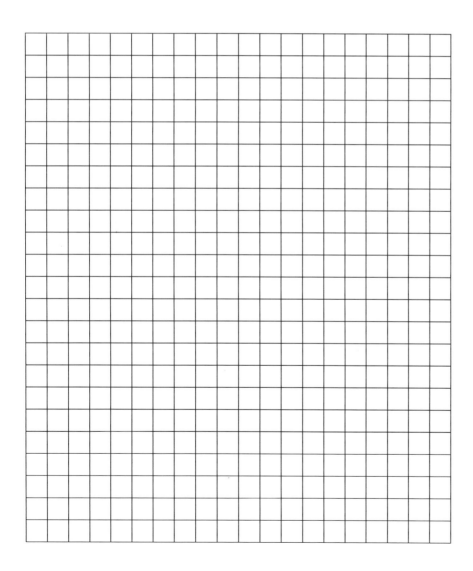

(6 marks)

19. A triangle ABC has coordinates A (1, 1), B (5, 1), C (3, 5).

(i) Sketch the triangle ABC on the grid below.

(1 mark)

(ii) The triangle PQR is a reflection of triangle ABC over the line x = -1.
Sketch triangle PQR on the same grid below.

(4 marks)

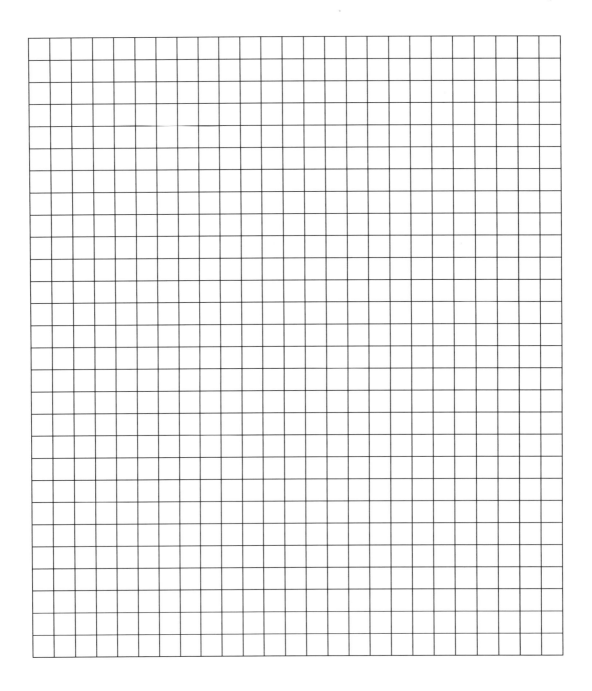

(total 5 marks)

20. Solve the following inequalities

   (i) $3(4x - 1) - 2(4x - 1) \leq 1$

(2 marks)

   (ii) $x^2 - 5x - 6 < 0$

(4 marks)

(total 6 marks)

21. Work out highest common factor and lowest common multiple of

   48, 80 and 108.

(4 marks)

Total for paper: 80 marks

End

GCSE Mathematics Paper 2 (calculator)

Higher Tier

Potential Paper E2

You must have: Ruler graduated in centimetres and millimetres, protractor, pair of compasses, pen, HB pencil, eraser.

Calculator is allowed

**Time allowed
1 hour and 30minutes
Total 80 marks**

Name

Date

1. (i) Expand and simplify $(2x - 1)(x + 3)(x - 1)$

(3marks)

(ii) Simplify $\left(\frac{2a^3b^2}{3c}\right)^3$

(2 marks)

(total 5 marks)

2. (i) Find highest common factor and lowest common multiple of 56 and 84.

(4 marks)

(ii) Highest common factor of A and B is 24. Write down two possible values for A and B.

(2 marks)

(total 6 marks)

3. Find the equation of line AB where A (2, -3) and B (5,0).

(3 marks)

4. A land is valued at £85,000 today. It is expected to increase in value by 6% each year. Calculate the expected value of the land in 3 years.

(2 marks)

5. a) complete the table below for $y = x^2 - 2x - 7$.

x	-2	-1	0	1	2	3	4
Y							

(2marks)

b) On the grid, draw the graph of $y = x^2 - 2x - 7$ for x values from -2 to 4.

(2 marks)

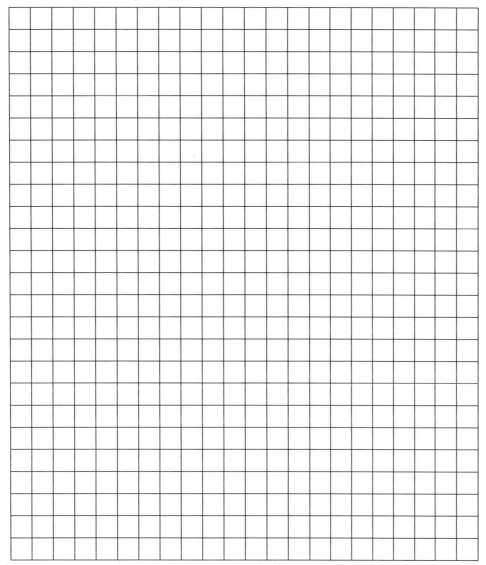

c) use your graph to estimate the solutions to equation

$$y = x^2 - 2x - 3$$

(2 marks)

(total 6 marks)

6. John ran 15km in 2 hours on day 1 and 24km in 3 hours on day 2. John has increased his speed by x% from day 1 to day 2. Find x?

(3 marks)

7. Triangle ABC is reflected to triangle PQR over the line x = -2.
   A (1, 4), B (1, 7), C (4, 4). Draw both triangles on the grid below.

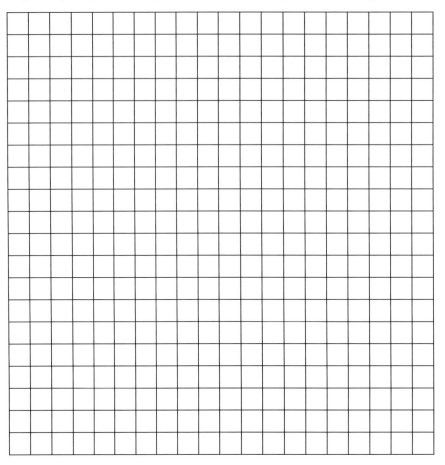

(3marks)

8. In a village 175 people took part in a survey. 127 of them had laptops and 83 had tablets. All 175 people had either a laptop or a tablet or both. Using a Venn diagram or otherwise, work out the probability of a randomly chosen person from this village having both a laptop and a tablet.

(4 marks)

9. Jenny had 120 sweets. She gave 20% to her parents and $\frac{7}{40}$ to her friends.

   From the rest, she ate 15 sweets.

   What percentage of her 120 sweets does she have now?

   (4 marks)

10. $\overrightarrow{AB} = \begin{pmatrix} 2 \\ 3 \\ 5 \end{pmatrix}$ and $\overrightarrow{AC} = \begin{pmatrix} 2 \\ -1 \\ 0 \end{pmatrix}$

Work out the following

(i) $3\overrightarrow{AC}$

   (1 mark)

(ii) $\overrightarrow{AC} - 2\overrightarrow{AB}$

   (3 marks)

11. Functions $t(x) = x + 5$ and $s(x) = 2x^2$.
    (i) Find st(x)

   (2 marks)

   (ii) Find tt(-3)

   (2 marks)
   (total 4 marks)

12. Y is proportional to x^2. When y is 96, x is 4.

  (i)   Find y, when x is -3.

(3 marks)

  (ii)   Find x, when y is 294.

(2 marks)

(total 5 marks)

13. AB and CD are diameters of a circle centred O and angle BAC is 53°.

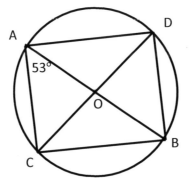

Work out

  (i)   Angle ADC

(2 marks)

  (ii)   Ange DOB

(2 marks)

  (iii) Angle ABC

(2 marks)

(total 6 marks)

14. An equation of a line is given by y = 2 – 3x.
   This equation meets the x – axis at P and y – axis at Q. Find coordinates
   of points P and Q.

   (3 marks)

15. There are m sweets in a bag. 8 of them are red and the rest are blue.
   Toby wants to eat two sweets at random one after the other. The
   probability of him eating two red sweets is $\frac{4}{15}$.

   (i)   Show that $m^2 - m - 210 = 0$

   (3 marks)

   (ii)   Hence, find the value of m?

   (2 marks)
   (total 5 marks)

16. Solve the following simultaneous equations.

    (i) $2x - 3y = 9$

            $5x - 4y = 19$

(3 marks)

    (ii) $x^2 + y^2 = 17$

          $y + x = 5$

(4 marks)

(total 7 marks)

17. Weight of 40 students are given below.

Weights (kg)	Frequency	Cumulative Frequency
40 - 50	6	
50 – 60	13	
60 – 70	10	
70 – 80	8	
80 -100	3	

(a) Draw a cumulative frequency graph.

(2 marks)

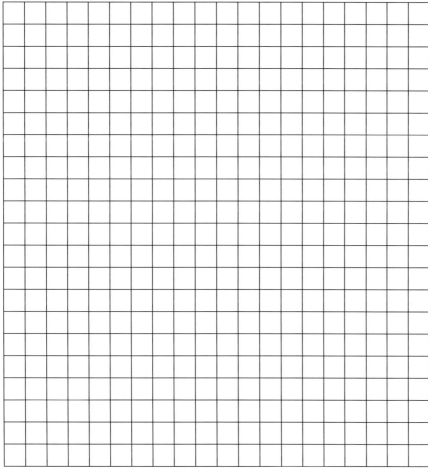

(b) Work out interquartile range.

(2 marks)

(total 4 marks)

18. Volume of the sphere is equal to the volume of the cone drawn below. Work out the value r?

Radius = 3 cm

Radius = r cm
Height = 8cm

(3 marks)

19. Rationalise the following surds.

(i) $\dfrac{12}{\sqrt{3}}$

(1 mark)

(ii) $\dfrac{8-\sqrt{2}}{\sqrt{2}}$

(2 marks)
(total 3 marks)

Total for paper: 80 marks

End

GCSE Mathematics Paper 3 (calculator)

Higher Tier

Potential Paper E3

You must have: Ruler graduated in centimetres and millimetres, protractor, pair of compasses, pen, HB pencil, eraser.

Calculator is allowed

**Time allowed
1 hour and 30minutes
Total 80 marks**

Name

Date

1. The table below shows sales figures of a company during a 5-year period.

Year	1	2	3	4	5
Sales (£1000's)	44	54	65	60	72

(i)   Plot the above figures on the grid below

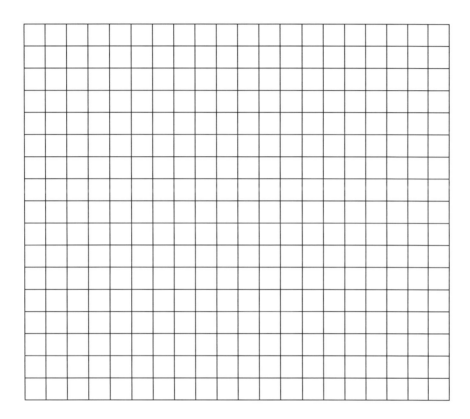

(1 mark)

(ii)   Using a best fit line, work out an estimate for the sales for year 6.

(1 mark)

(iii)   What type of a correlation does this show?

(1 mark)

(total 3 marks)

2. (i) Complete the square for $x^2 - 6x + 1$

(2 marks)

(ii) Hence, show that the solution to $x^2 - 6x + 1$ is $3 \pm 2\sqrt{2}$

(2 marks)

(total 4 marks)

3. A trapezium has vertices A (2, 1), B (10, 1), C (3, 6) & D (7, 6).
   (i)   Draw the trapezium ABCD on the grid below

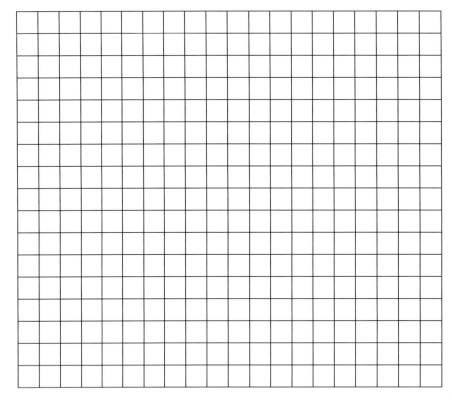

(2 marks)

   (ii)   A triangle has an area of exactly half the area of the trapezium
          ABCD. If the triangle has a height of 5 units, work out its base.

(3 marks)

(total 5 marks)

4. A bag has 4 red counters and 3 green counters. A counter is taken at random to check the colour and replaced. Then a second counter is also taken to check the colour.
Calculate the probability of at least picking one red counter out of the two counters.

(3 marks)

5. Calculate the area of triangle ABC.

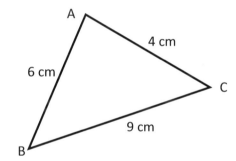

(4 marks)

6. A, B & C shared £126 in ratio 7:9:5. A gave £6 to B. Work out the new ratio?

(4 marks)

7. Solve the following

$$\frac{x^2}{3x - 8} = 2$$

(3 marks)

8. Find a and b. (give reasons for each stage)

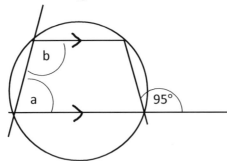

(4 marks)

9. $P = 0.00125$, $Q = 2.5 \times 10^5$

   (i)   Write P in standard form

                                             (1 mark)

   (ii)   Write Q in ordinary form

                                             (1 mark)

   (iii)   Work out $\dfrac{\sqrt{Q}}{P}$ in standard form.

                                             (2 marks)

                                        (total 4 marks)

10. A station is open from 6am to midnight. Trains to A & to B depart together at 6am from the station. However, trains to A run every 25 mins and trains to B run every 40 minutes.
How many times a day do trains to A and B depart at the same time from this station?

                                             (3 marks)

11. Sofia invested £3000 for 5 years in a bank. Bank has the following offer.

5.5% compound interest for first 2 years
3% compound interest for remaining years

Calculate the amount of interest Sofia will earn at the end of 5 years.

(3 marks)

12. Company A has annual costs of £y-thousand in x years.
It follows the formula $y = 5x + 3$

Company B initially had a cost of £4000 and costs increased at a rate 20% less than the rate of company A.

Calculate the difference between the costs of companies A & B in the 3rd year.

(4 marks)

13. In the diagram below PQ is parallel to BC.

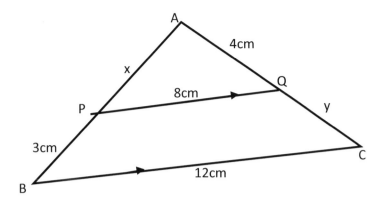

(i) Prove that triangle ABC is mathematically similar to triangle APQ.

(1 mark)

(ii) Work out values x and y.

(3 marks)

(total 4 marks)

14. Average age of 24 students is 16.5 and when the 25th student joined the group, average age decreased to 16.4.
Work out the age of the 25th student.

(3 marks)

15. $y = x^2$

(i)   Plot the above graph on the grid below for x values from 0 to 5.

X	0	1	2	3	4	5
y						

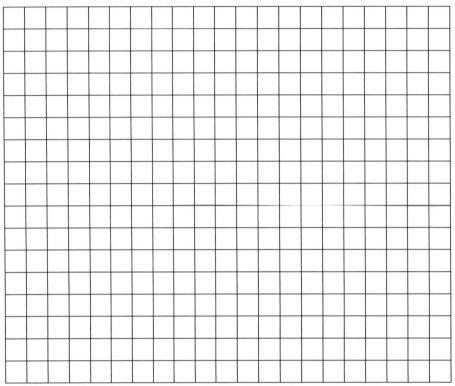

(2 marks)

(ii)   Work out an estimate for the area under the graph between x = 1 and x =4. (use 3 strips of equal width)

(3 marks)

(iii) Is your estimate to part (ii) an underestimate or an overestimate?

(1 mark)

(total 6 marks)

16.a) The nth term of a sequence is given by $xn^2 - yn$. Where x and y are integers. Second term of the sequence is 16 and the fifth term is 115. Find the eight term of the sequence.

(4 marks)

b) Here are the first 5 terms of a different quadratics sequence.

-1, 0, 3, 8, 15

Find an expression for the nth term of the sequence.

(2 marks)

(total 6 marks)

17. Diagram below shows the sector AOB of radius 6cm & line AB is 5cm.

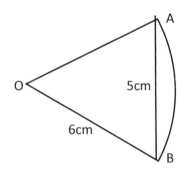

(i)   Work out arc length AB.

(3 marks)

(ii)   Hence, find the perimeter of sector OAB.

(1 mark)

(total 4 marks)

18.a) Show that $x^5 + 2x = 100$ has a solution between 2 and 3.

(2 marks)

b) Show that the equation $x^5 + 2x = 100$ can be rearranged to give

$$x = \sqrt[5]{100 - 2x}$$

(1 mark)

c) Starting with $x_0 = 2.4$.

Use the formula $x_{n+1} = \sqrt[5]{100 - 2x_n}$ three times to estimate the solution of $x^5 + 2x = 100$ to 3 decimal places.

(3 marks)
(total 6 marks)

19. 50 members of a sports club were surveyed to check if they like cross country running, archery and basketball.

25 like cross country running

3 like all three

7 like cross country running and archery only

8 like cross country running and basketball

6 like basketball only

5 like archery and basketball

10 do not like all three

(i)   Draw a Venn diagram

(2 marks)

(ii)   How many people like archery?

(2 marks)

(iii)   What is the probability that a member likes exactly two of these?

(3 marks)

(total 7 marks)

Total for paper: 80 marks

End

Section F

GCSE Mathematics Paper 1 (non-calculator)

Higher Tier

Potential Paper F1

You must have: Ruler graduated in centimetres and millimetres, protractor, pair of compasses, pen, HB pencil, eraser.

Calculator is not allowed

Time allowed
1 hour and 30minutes
Total 80 marks

Name

Date

1. Plot y = 2x – 3 for x values from -3 to 3.

X	-3	-2	-1	0	1	2	3
y							

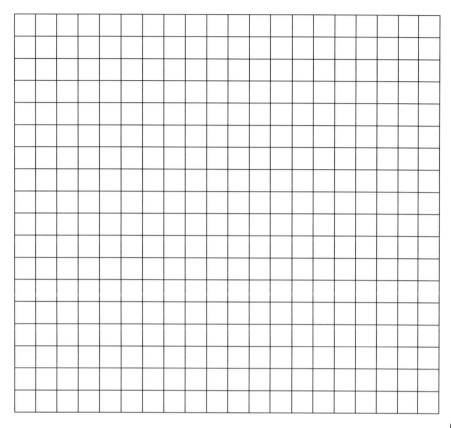

(3 marks)

2. a) Express 135 as a product of its prime factors.

(2 marks)

b) Work out highest common factor and lowest common multiple of 135 and 180.

(3 marks)
(total 5 marks)

3. work out

   (i) 5.12×2.9

(2 marks)

   (ii) $4\frac{1}{2} \div 7\frac{3}{4}$

(2 marks)

(total 4 marks)

4. A cylinder has radius $x$cm and height $h$cm. The volume of the cylinder is $192\pi cm^3$. Show that the surface area of the solid cylinder is

$$\left(2\pi x^2 + \frac{384\pi}{x}\right) cm^2$$

(4 marks)

5. A metal frame ABCD has 4 metal bars as shown in the diagram.
   AD = DC, angle BAD = angle ABD and angle ABC is a right angle.
   1 metre of metal bars cost £15.50.
   Calculate the cost of the frame ABCD.

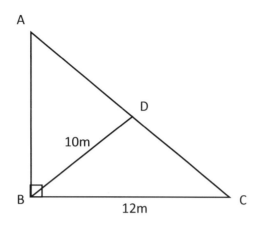

(5 marks)

6. Line l_1 has equation y = 3 - 2x. Line l_2 is perpendicular to Line l_1 and passes through the point (1, 4).

   Find equation of Line l_2.

(4 marks)

7. a) Draw a cumulative frequency graph for following data.

Height (cm)	Frequency	Cumulative Frequency
140-160	3	
160-170	7	
170-190	8	
190-200	4	
200-220	2	

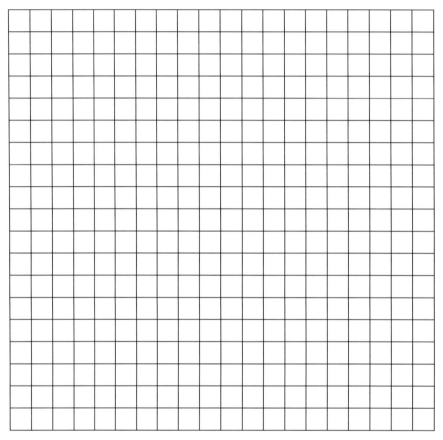

(2 marks)

b) Work out the median height.

(1 mark)

c) Estimate the number of people taller than 175cm.

(2 marks)

(total 5 marks)

8. (i) Write 0.000274 in standard form.

(1 mark)

(iii) work out the value of $(1.92 \times 10^{-2}) \div (1.28 \times 10^{-5})$
(write your answer in standard form)

(2marks)

(total 3 marks)

9. David bought a bike for £X. The value of the bike decreases by 10% each year. After 2 years his bike is worth £4050.
Find X?

(3 marks)

10. Expand $(x - 3)^3$

(3 marks)

11. $y = x^2 - 4x + 1$

(i)   Complete the table below

x	-1	0	1	2	3	4	5
y							

(1mark)

(ii)   Hence, plot $y = x^2 - 4x + 1$ for x values between -1 and 5.

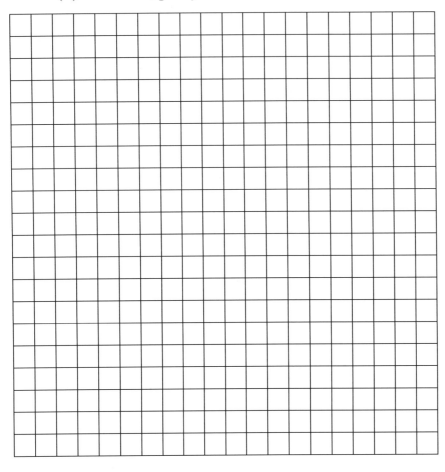

(2 marks)

(iii)   Use your graph to solve

$$y = x^2 - 4x - 2$$

(2 marks)

(total 5 marks)

12. Work out
    (i) $(32)^{-1/5}$

(2 marks)

    (ii) $\left(\frac{8}{27}\right)^{-4/3}$

(3 marks)

(total 5 marks)

13. A is inversely proportional to B^2. When A is 12, B is 3.
    Work out B, when A is 3.

(3 marks)

14. The ratios of A:B =3:4 & B:C = 2:3.
    A, B & C shared £x between them. C received £75 more than A.
    Find x.

(3 marks)

15. The volume of a sphere is equal to the volume of a cylinder whose radius is 2cm and height is 5cm. Work out the radius of the sphere.

(4 marks)

16. Prove algebraically that $n^2 - n$ is always an even number for all integers n.

(4 marks)

17. There are 4 mangos and 5 pears in a bag.
    John and Mary ate one fruit each.
    Work out the probability of them eating at least one mango.

(4 marks)

18. Maggie cooks rice about 3 to 4 times a week. 1kg of rice costs 85 pence and she uses 200 grams per serving.
    Calculate an estimate for the amount of money she spends on rice every month.

(3 marks)

19. $\overrightarrow{OA} = a$ and $\overrightarrow{OB} = b$, $AC:CB = 5:2$ and D is midpoint of OA

Work out $\overrightarrow{DC}$.

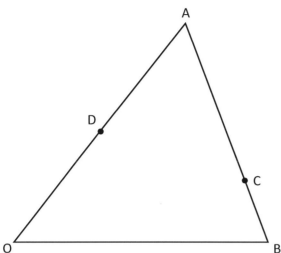

(4 marks)

20. Solve the following equations

   (i) $x^2 - y^2 = 11$

           $y - 2x = 17$

(4 marks)

   (ii) $3^{x+1} \times 3^{2x} = 3^{13}$

(2 marks)

(total 6 marks)

Total for paper: 80 marks

End

GCSE Mathematics
Paper 2
(calculator)

Higher
Tier

Potential Paper F2

You must have: Ruler graduated in centimetres and millimetres, protractor, pair of compasses, pen, HB pencil, eraser.

Calculator is allowed

Time allowed
1 hour and 30minutes
Total 80 marks

Name

Date

1. The table shows the probabilities of events A, B, C, D and E.

Event	A	B	C	D	E
Probability	0.1		0.35		0.07

B is 3 times as likely as D.

A sample of 750 events were taken. Work out the number of events B or D in the sample.

(3 marks)

2. 50 girls and boys were asked, what they had in the mid-morning break out of fruits, chocolates and sandwiches. There were 23 girls in the group. Out of 18 people who had fruits, 11 were girls. 9 boys had chocolates and 8 girls had sandwiches.

Work out the percentage of girls who had chocolates.

(4 marks)

3. A water tank is 10m x 5m x 3m. A model of the tank is designed to a scale of 2cm to 1m. Calculate the volume of the model.

(3 marks)

4. Brenda drove from city A to city B. She left A at 9am. She drove 75km at 60km/h and stopped for a 20 minutes break. She then drove another 50km at 75km/h and reached city B.
Work out the time of her arrival at B.

(3 marks)

5. QR is parallel to ST. Work out x & y.

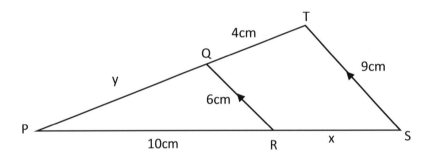

(4 marks)

6. A lorry is bought for £35,000 brand new. It is expected to depreciate in value by 18% per year.
   Work out its value after 4 years?

(3 marks)

7. A = 2.5 (correct to one decimal place)
   B = 100 (correct to one significant figure)
   (i)   Write down limits of accuracy for A & B.

(2 marks)

(ii)   Calculate the lower bund for $\dfrac{B-A}{3A}$

(2 marks)

(total 4 marks)

8. Draw a histogram for following data.

Ages	Frequency	Frequency Density
10-14	2	
14-18	10	
18-20	3	
20-30	1	

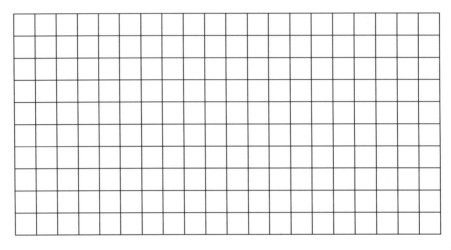

(3 marks)

9. The triangle ABC has coordinates A (-1, 2), B (-1, 5), C (2,5)
   (i)   Sketch the triangle ABC

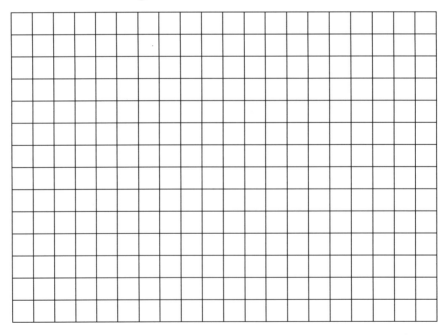

(1mark)

   (ii)   Translate triangle ABC by vector $\begin{pmatrix} 3 \\ -2 \end{pmatrix}$

(3 marks)
(total 4 marks)

10. Write these in ascending order

$$234 \times 10^{-2}, \quad 2.34 \times 10^{-2}, \quad 23.4 \times 10^{-2}, \quad 0.234 \times 10^{-2}$$

(2 marks)

11. Solve the following equation

$$\frac{x+1}{2x-1} = \frac{x+3}{3x-1}$$

(4 marks)

12. There are 20 students in a class. 12 are boys and 8 are girl. The teacher randomly picks 2 students.

(i)   Represent all probabilities on a tree diagram.

(2 marks)

(ii)   Work out probability of picking one girl and one boy in any order.

(2 marks)

(iii)   Work out probability of picking at least one boy.

(2 marks)

(total 6 marks)

13. Solve the following inequalities
    (i) $2x - 7 \leq 18$

(2 marks)

    (ii) $2x^2 - 7x - 15 > 0$

(3 marks)

(total 5 marks)

14. PQ is a tangent at C to a circle centred at O.
A & B are two points on the circumference of the circle.
Angle PCA = 68° and AC = AB.

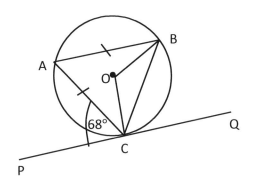

Work out the following. (give reasons for each stage)

(i)   Angle BCQ

(3 marks)

(ii)   Angle OCB

(2 marks)
(total 5 marks)

15. Prove using algebra that $0.2\dot{4}\dot{5} \times 0.\dot{7} = \frac{21}{110}$

(3 marks)

16. Sector OPQ is drawn below. PQ = 10cm and angle POQ = 24°.

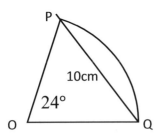

(i) Calculate arc length PQ.

(3 marks)

(ii) Calculate the area of sector OPQ.

(2 marks)

(total 5 marks)

17. Work out the exact value of x.

$$4^{2x+1} \times 2^{3x-1} = 32^{\frac{2}{5}}$$

(3 marks)

18. Simply the following.

(i) $\dfrac{2}{2x+3} - \dfrac{1}{3x-5}$

(2 marks)

(ii) $\dfrac{4x^2-1}{2x^2-3x-2}$

(3 marks)

(total 5 marks)

19. Equation of a circle is $x^2 + y^2 = 25$ & P $(3, 4)$ is a point on the circle.

(i) Find an equation of the tangent to circle at P.

(3 marks)

(ii) Above tangent meets x-axis at A and y-axis at B. Work out the area of the triangle OAB where O is the origin.

(3 marks)

(total 6 marks)

20. $y = x^2 + 4x - 1$

   (i)   Draw $y = x^2 + 4x - 1$ on the grid below for x values from -6 to 2.

X	-6	-5	-4	-3	-2	-1	0	1
y								

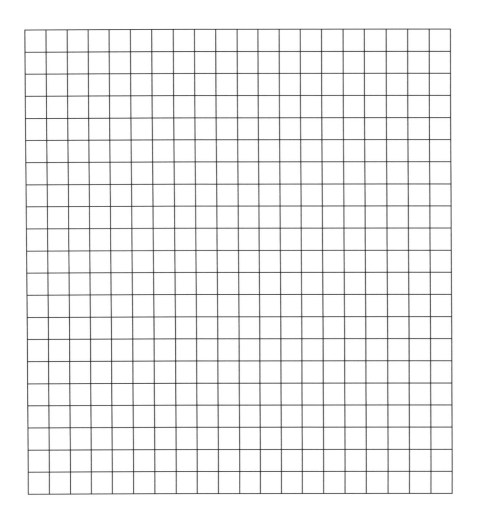

(3 marks)

   (ii)   Use your graph to solve $x^2 + 4x - 1 = 0$

(2 marks)

(total 5 marks)

Total for paper: 80 marks

End

GCSE Mathematics
Paper 3
(calculator)

Higher
Tier

Potential Paper F3

You must have: Ruler graduated in centimetres and millimetres, protractor, pair of compasses, pen, HB pencil, eraser.

Calculator is allowed

Time allowed
1 hour and 30minutes
Total 80 marks

Name

Date

1. There are 50 students in a school sixth form.

   35 study mathematics, 24 study physics and 5 people do not study mathematics nor physics.

   (i) Using a Venn diagram or otherwise, work out the number of people who study both subjects.

   (4 marks)

   (ii) Calculate the probability of a student studying only mathematics.

   (2 marks)

   (total 6 marks)

2. Solve the following

$$xy = 18$$
$$y - x = 3$$

   (4 marks)

3. Table below shows the weight of puppies one week after they were born.

Weight (grams)	Frequency		
100-400	1		
400-600	3		
600-700	7		
700-800	2		
800-1000	1		

(i) Write down the modal class

(1 mark)

(ii) Write down the median class

(1 mark)

(iii) Work out the mean weight

(2 marks)

(iv) Represent the data on a frequency polygon

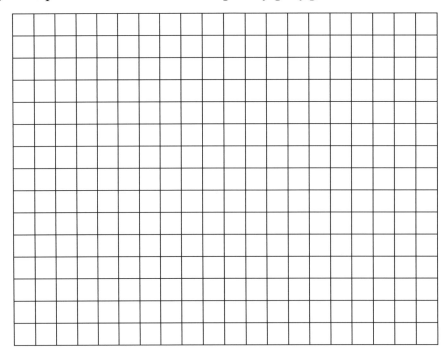

(2 marks)

(total 6 marks)

4. David has £240. He gave $\frac{1}{6}$ to his sister and 20% to his parents. He spent £32 from the remaining balance. He then shared the rest with his friend Ben in the ratio as follows.
David : Ben = 3:2

Calculate the amount received by Ben.

(4 marks)

5. Work out the sum of interior angles of a decagon.

(2 marks)

6. Liquid A has density $2.4 g/cm^3$ and liquid B has density $1.8\ g/cm^3$. $200ml$ of A is mixed with $120ml$ of B.
Work out the density of the mixture.

(3 marks)

7. Calculate the area of triangle LMN to two decimal places.

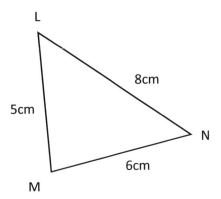

(3 marks)

8. A rectangle has a width of 8.2 cm. The area of this rectangle is equal to the area of a circle whose radius is 7.5 cm.
Work out the perimeter of the rectangle.
(write your answer to one decimal place)

(3 marks)

9. Mike invested £4000 for 5 years in a bank. Bank pays x% compound interest for first 2 years and 3% compound interest for remaining years.
His balance after the 5-year period was £4818.93.
Find x?

(4 marks)

10. Marks for an examination has the following information.

	Lowest	Lower Quartile	Median	Upper Quartile	Highest
Girls	42	55	61	71	97
Boys	30	49	52	65	99

(i)   Draw a box blots for both girls and boys.

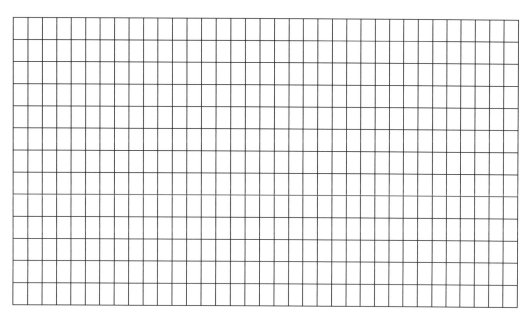

(2 marks)

(ii)   Compare both girls and boys marks.

(2 marks)

(total 4 marks)

11. Two points A and B are such that A (1, 4) & B(3, -4).
    Work out
    (i)   Midpoint of AB

(1 mark)

    (ii)   Equation of line AB

(3 marks)

    (iii)   Equation of perpendicular line to AB through its midpoint

(3 marks)

(total 7 marks)

12.a) Simplify

$$\frac{18x^2 - 2}{3x^2 - 4x + 1}$$

(3 marks)

b) Make b the subject of the formula

$$a = \frac{\sqrt{b^2 + ac}}{b}$$

(3 marks)

(total 6 marks)

13. Triangle PQR is right angled at Q. Work out x.

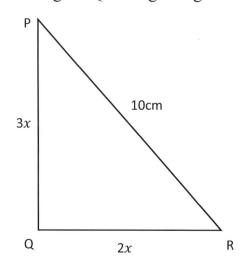

(3 marks)

14. Shade the region bounded by these inequalities.

$$x + y \leq 4, \qquad y > 2x + 1, \qquad y > -1$$

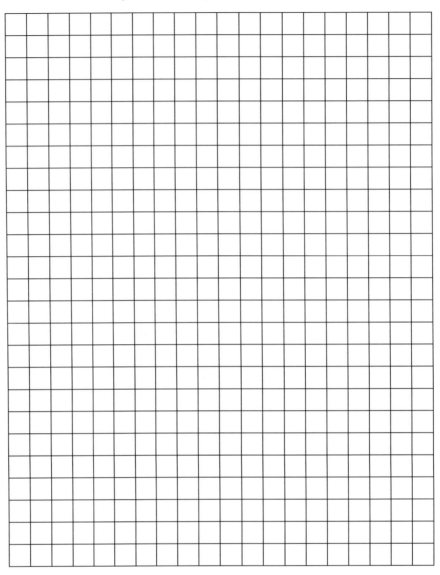

(4 marks)

15. $x^2 - x - 1 = 0$

    (i)   Show that there is a root for above equation between 1 and 2.

(2 marks)

    (ii)   Rearrange the equation, so that

$$x = \sqrt[3]{x + 1}$$

(1 mark)

    (iii)   Using

$$x_{n+1} = \sqrt[3]{x_n + 1} \text{ with } x_0 = 1.5$$

        Calculate x_1, x_2, x_3 to 4 decimal places.

(3 marks)

(6 marks)

16. Force A is 25N (correct to nearest Newton). Force A is applied to an area of $0.5m^2$ (correct to 1 decimal place)

$$Pressure = \frac{Force}{Area}$$

Work out the upper bound for the pressure applied by force A.

(3 marks)

17. AC is a tangent to the circle at A. O is the centre of the circle.

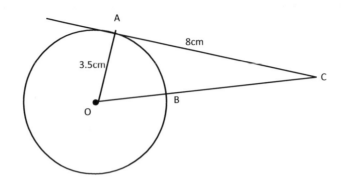

OA = 3.5cm, AC = 8cm & line OC meets the circle at B.

(i)   Work out the length BC.

(2 marks)

(ii)   Calculate the area enclosed by AC, BC & arc AB.

(3 marks)

(5 marks)

18. Solve the following equations
   (i) $5x^2 - 7x - 6 = 0$ by factorising

(2 marks)

   (ii) $x^2 - 14x + 9 = 0$ by completing the square

(3 marks)

   (iii) $4x^2 + 7x - 1 = 0$ using quadratic formula

(2 marks)
(total 7 marks)

Total for paper: 80 marks

End

Answers

Section A – Paper 1	**Section A – Paper 2**	**Section A – Paper 3**
1. $-4 \leq x < 2$	1. a) x^{17} b) i) $28x^2 - 27x - 10$ ii) $4y^2 - 12y + 9$	1. $AC = 12.49cm$ $AB = 26.60cm$
2. HCF=48, LCM=576		2. i) -1.44, ii) 6.86
3. $x = £600, y = 6$	2. Sketch with coordinates $(0,-3), (3,0)$ & $(-1,0)$	3. $x = \frac{5+y}{3y-2}$
4. a) i) 4.07×10^5, ii) 4.07×10^{-2} b) 1.25×10^{-2}	3. i) 236, ii) 8.66	4. £37.24
	4. $y = -\frac{2}{5}x + \frac{11}{5}$	5. correct frequency polygon
5. $1260°$	5. £111.57	6. $2m/s^2$
6. $2:3$	6. No with evidence	7. $3cm$
7. correctly plotted graph	7. i) 18 ii) ± 12	8. 12 $miles$
8. 63	8. correct plots	9. $\frac{10}{7}$
9. $288\pi cm^3$	9. $\frac{19}{30}$	10. 10
10. correct proof	10. i) correct proof ii) $2.20cm$	11. $31.1°$
11. median £590 & I.Q.R £170	11. $4.2°$	12. i) $2x(3x+1)(3x-1)$ ii) $(2x-15)(x+2)$
12. 0.18	12. i) 9 ii) $\frac{x+1}{2}$ iii) 17	13. Correct proof $RT = 9cm$
13. Train with reasons	13. correct proof	14. $7.84cm$
14. $2c - \frac{3}{2}a$	14. $x < -\frac{4}{3}$ & $x > 2$	15. $48.2°$
15. i) 48, ii) ± 7	15. $x = 5$	16. correct histogram
16. $4\frac{1}{4}$	16. $when$ $x = 3, y = 9$ $when$ $x = -\frac{27}{5}, y = -\frac{39}{5}$	17. $x = 6$
17. $x = -1$ or $\frac{21}{8}$	17. correct proof	18. i) $show$ $sign$ $change$ ii) $correct$ $proof$ iii) $x_1 = 4.2818$ $x_2 = 4.2296$
18. $y = -\frac{12}{5}x + \frac{196}{5}$		19. $when$ $x = 3, y = 16$ $when$ $x = -\frac{16}{3}, y = -9$

Section B – Paper 1	Section B – Paper 2	Section B – Paper 3
1. $2\frac{4}{33}$	1. $30.2cm^2$	1. $i)\frac{10y^5}{3x^7}$, $ii)\frac{16a^8}{81b^{12}}$
2. 20%	2. 63.9	2. $73.575cm^2$
3. correct proof	3. $a = 18, b = -2$	3. $i)$ 86400, $ii)$ 8.64×10^4
4. 135°	4. $41.10cm^2$	4. correct plot
5. $i. y = 5, ii. x = 7, y = 3,$ $iii. x = 8 \; or \; x = 3$	5. $2.5ms^{-2}$	5. 24
6. 6:5	6. $i)$ 20.1, $ii)$ 5×10^{10}	6. £60
7. 0.3	7. $x = 5$	7. correct plot and enlargement
8. 1200	8. Tony is better value	8. $i)$ $x = 2, y = 1,$ $ii)\frac{2x}{x-2}$
9. $\frac{36}{25}$	9. $4000g$	9. $i)$ correct tree diagram $ii)\frac{5}{7}$
10. £156	10. $y = 3.43cm$	10. Van is faster with reasons
11. $2n^2 + 3n$	11. correct proof	11. £1365
12. 40° $with \; reasons$	12. $\frac{19}{66}$	12. correct proof
13. $x = 5 \; or \; x - 4$	13. $i)12cm, ii)$ $6cm$	13. 5.83 or 0.17
14. $A:B = 1:2$	14. $B = \pm6$	14. correct sketch
15. $y = 2x + 7$	15. $i)$ $2x^2(2x - 5),$ $ii)$ $(2x - 3)(3x - 2),$ $iii)$ $(4x + 3y)(4x - 3y)$	15. $x^2 + 8x + 16$
16. $i)$ $3\sqrt{3} - 1, ii)$ $5\sqrt{3},$ $iii)$ $3\sqrt{2} + 1$	16. $i)m = 4, ii)y = -\frac{1}{4}x$	16. $53.69cm^2$
17. $a = \frac{5}{2}, b = \frac{-21}{4}$	17. $i.$ correct plot $ii.$ correct reflection	17. $i)$ correct proof $ii)$ $x_1 = 2.9625, x_2 = 2.9368$
18. $y = x^2 - 3x - 10$	18. $S\hat{O}R = 136°,$ $P\hat{Q}S = 22°$ & $P\hat{R}S = 22°$ with correct reasons.	18. correct histogram
19. $x = 1$		19. $\frac{1}{10}(6b - a)$
		20. $r = 5.21cm$

Section C – Paper 1	Section C – Paper 2	Section C – Paper 3
1. $27a^{15}b^9$	1. i) $x \geq \frac{1}{2}$	1. $5450 \leq A < 5550$
	ii) $-1 < x < 4$ with a sketch	$20.45 \leq B < 20.55$
2. i) 13, ii) 12	2. $B\hat{R}S = x + y$	2. £860
	(*alternate angles*)	
3. £150	3. £398,462.02	3. Histogram drawn
4. $132cm^2$	4. £6000.30	4. $20°$
5. i)6m/s, ii) 21.6km/s	5. 5×10^2	5. i) 5.86cm, ii) $51.3°$
6. $x = 2, y = 3$	6. i) (3,10)	6. 6.87cm
	ii) $y = 5x - 5$	
7. $HCF = 21, LCM = 420$	7. i), ii) plot and rotation	7. i) $6x^3 - 19x^2 + x + 6$
		ii) $x^2 + 7x + 5$
8. a) 1/2, b) $6\sqrt{2}$cm	8. $37.60cm^2$	8. £382.01
9. frequency polygon drawn	9. i) tree diagram, ii) $\frac{2}{3}$	9. sketch shown
10. a) $\frac{2x-3}{x+1}$, b) $(a-b)(4a+3b)$	10. i) 163cm,	10. i) $314.16cm^3$,
	ii) Interquartile Range 19cm	ii) $282.74cm^2$
11. $2\frac{5}{26}$	iii) 17.5%	11. i) show a sign change
	11. i) 19.32cm, ii) $4.40cm^2$	ii) 2.0801,2.1105,2.1218
12. $x = 38°$		12. i)12, ii) ± 7
	12. a) $\frac{3x-7}{x^2-3x+2}$, b) $x = 3$	
13. i) & ii) plot & translation		13. proof shown
	13. 6.86cm	
14. a) $\frac{9}{25}$, b) $x = 4$		14. $21.86cm^2$
	14. $x = \frac{y+2}{2y-3}$	
15. i) $288\pi x m^3$, ii) 32cm		15. $3.2g/cm\wedge3$
	15. $66°$	
16. i)$\frac{3}{10}$, ii) $\frac{1}{3}$, iii) $\frac{1}{30}$, iv) $\frac{13}{99}$	16. £450	16. 4.55cm
		17. $3n^2 - 5n + 1$
17. $a = 5, b = -22$	17. $27.81cm^2$	
		18. $x = 7, y = 3$
18. Plot shown	18.$\frac{1}{6}(4b - a)$	
		19. $y = \frac{2}{3}x + 3$
19. Proof shown		

Section D – Paper 1

1. a) $2 \times 2 \times 2 \times 2 \times 3$
b) $HCF = 24, LCM = 144$
2. 85

3. proof shown

4. 20%

5. i)3.27816, ii) 40

6. proof shown

7. plot shown

8. $-x^2, x^0, x^{\frac{2}{3}}, x^{\frac{3}{2}}, (-x)^2$

9. i) 0.0002,
ii) 2,000,000,000
10. i) 2, ii) $\frac{25}{36}$

11. $a = 7, b = 3$

12. i)50-60, ii)50-60
iii)frequency polygon drawn
13. i) 45, ii) 27

14. $x = 15, y = 25$

15. proof shown

16. $n = 90$

17. proof shown

18. i) $\left(4, \frac{13}{2}\right)$
ii) $y = -\frac{4}{7}x + \frac{123}{14}$
19. $\frac{7+4\sqrt{2}}{7}$

Section D – Paper 2

1. i)$x = 12$,
ii) $x = -\frac{3}{2}, x = 4$
2. £306267.75

3. 7.7cm

4. $\frac{2}{3}$

5. i) & ii) plot and translation shown
6. a)$x = 2$, b)$8a^9b^{-6}$

7. 37.8°

8. upper 2.78, lower 2.09

9. £3240

10. 324km

11. 66.6%

12. 5

13. Bank B with reasons

14. i) $x < \frac{17}{4}$,
ii) $-2 < x < 5$ with sketch
15. 15

16. 14.86 & 1.14

17. i) curve drawn, ii) £3000
iii) £3500
18. $6\sqrt{2}$

19. i)$f^{-1}(x) = \frac{x-1}{3}$,
ii) $fg(x) = 6x - 8$
iii) gf(3)=17
20. $1.77cm^2$

Section D – Paper 3

1. histogram drawn.

2. £11.72

3. 51.7km/h

4. 11 years

5. i) $(2, -2)$,
ii) $y = \frac{1}{8}x - \frac{9}{4}$
6. $45.84cm^2$

7. a) 9, b) 476

8. 0.1513

9. No with reasons

10. 0.031

11. i) $3x(x - 4)$,
ii) $2a(7a + 4)$
iii) $(y + 10)(y - 10)$
iv) $(x - 10)(x + 3)$
v) $(x - 5)(3x + 2)$
12. proof shown

13. i) tree diagram drawn
ii) 0.325
iii) 0.7
14. proof shown

15. 2.57 & -0.91

16. 523.25g

17. 11.37cm

18. i) $b - a$, ii) $\frac{2}{5}(b - a)$

19. i) plot shown
ii) intersections of graphs

Section E – Paper 1

1. $1\frac{2}{3}$

2. i) $4n + 9$, ii) 309, iii) No

3. £5600

4. 2160

5. $150cm^2$

6. i) $\left(3, -\frac{1}{2}\right)$, ii) $\frac{3}{2}$, iii) $y = 2x - \frac{13}{2}$

7. construction shown

8. $540\pi cm^3$

9. i) 25, ii) 1, iii) $\frac{27}{8}$

10. $x = 4$

11. $71°$

12. proof shown

13. $a = 2, b = 15$

14. $B = 1/4$

15. i) $2x(x - 4)(x + 1)$ ii) $x((x + 1)(x - 1)$

16. 0.9775

17. $\frac{16x-3}{(2x-3)(5x+3)}$

18. i) & ii) sketches shown

19. i) & ii) sketches shown

20. i) $x \leq \frac{1}{2}$ ii) $-1 < x < 6$

Section E – Paper 2

1. i) $2x^3 + 3x^2 - 8x + 3$ ii) $\dfrac{8a^9b^6}{27c^3}$

2. i) $HCF = 14$, $LCM = 168$ ii) 48 & 72 or any other

3. $y = x - 5$

4. £101236.36

5. i) & ii) table and plot shown

6. 6.7%

7. drawing shown

8. $\frac{1}{5}$

9. 50%

10. i) $\begin{matrix} 6 & -4 \\ 0 & -10 \end{matrix}$, ii) -3, -7

11. i) $2(x + 5)^2$, ii) 7

12. i) 54, ii) ± 7

13. i) $37°$, ii) $74°$, iii) $37°$

14. $\frac{P92}{3}, 0)$, $Q(0,2)$

15. i) proof shown, ii) m = 15

16. i) $x = 3, y = -1$ ii) $x = \pm 4, y = \pm 1$

17. i) curve drawn, ii)17kg

18. 3.67cm

19. i) $4\sqrt{2}$, ii) $4\sqrt{2} - 1$

Section E – Paper 3

1. i) scatter graph shown ii) £80000, iii) positive

2. i) $(x - 3)^2 - 8$ ii) proof shown

3. i) sketch shown ii) 12cm

4. $\frac{41}{49}$

5. $9.54cm^2$

6. $6 : 10 : 5$

7. $x = 4$ or $x = 2$

8. $a = 85°, b = 95°$

9. i) 1.25×10^{-3} ii) 250000, iii) 4×10^5

10. 6 times

11. £3648.70

12. £2000

13. i) proof shown ii) $x = 6cm, y = 2cm$

14. 14 years old

15. i) 21-25 unit squared ii) an overestimate

16. $x = 5$, ii)$n^2 - 2n$

17. i) 5.15cm, ii) 17.15cm

18. a) change of sign shown b) proof shown, c) 2.486

19. i) Venn diagram drawn ii) 19, iii) $\frac{7}{20}$

Section F – Paper 1	Section F – Paper 2	Section F – Paper 3
1. plot shown	1. 360	1. $i)14, ii)\frac{21}{50}$
2. $a) 3 \times 3 \times 3 \times 5$ b) $HCF = 45, LCM = 540$	2. 8%	2. $y = 6$
3. $i) 14.848, ii)\frac{18}{31}$	3. $1200cm^3$	3. i) 600-700, ii) 600-700, iii) 621.4g, iv) freq. poly.
4. proof shown	4. 11.15am	4. £48
5. £899	5. $x = 5cm, y = 8cm$	5. $144°$
6. $y = \frac{1}{2}x + \frac{7}{2}$	6. £15824.26	6. $2.175g/cm^3$
7. i) curve drawn ii) median = 174cm, iii) 11	7. $i) 2.45 \leq A < 2.55$ $50 \leq B < 150, ii) 6.20$	7. $14.98cm^2$
8. $i) 2.74 \times 10^{-4}$, $ii) 1.5 \times 10^3$	8. Histogram drawn	8. 59.5cm
9. £5000	9. sketch and translation shown	9. 5
10. $x^3 - 9x + 27x - 27$	10. $order$ 4,2,3,1	10. I.Q.R is same for both Girls range is smaller Girls have a higher median
11. i) table completed ii)plot shown iii) solve using plot	11. $x = 3, x = 1$	11. $i)(2,0), ii) y = -4x + 8$ $iii)y = \frac{1}{4}x - \frac{1}{2}$
12. $i)\frac{1}{2}, ii)\frac{81}{16}$	12. i) tree diagram drawn ii) $\frac{48}{95}, iii)\frac{81}{95}$	12. $a)\ \frac{2(3x+1)}{x-1}, b)\ \sqrt{\frac{ac}{a^2-1}}$
13. $B = \pm 6$	13. $i) x \leq \frac{25}{2}$ $ii) x < -\frac{3}{2}, x > 5$	13. 2.77cm
14. £325	14. $i) 44°, ii) 46°$	14. correct region shaded
15. 2.47cm	15. $proof\ shown$	15. $i)\ change\ of\ sign$ ii) proof shown iii)1.3572,1.3309,1.3259
16. proof shown	16.i)10.07cm, ii) $121.14cm^2$	16. $56.7N/m^2$
17. $\frac{13}{18}$	17. $x = \frac{1}{7}$	17. $i) 5.23cm, ii) 6.90cm^2$
18. £2.30 to £2.50	18. $\frac{2x-1}{x-2}$	18. $i) x = 2, -\frac{3}{5}$ $ii) 7 + 2\sqrt{10}, 7 - 2\sqrt{10}$ $iii) 0.133, -1.88$
19. $\frac{1}{14}(10b - 3a)$	19. $i) y = -\frac{3}{4}x + \frac{25}{4}$ $ii)\frac{625}{24}$	
20. $i) x = -6, y = -6$ $ii) x = 4$	20. i) plot shown ii) solve using the plot	

Printed in Great Britain
by Amazon

32797152R00132